THE EAGLE AND
THE DOVE

By the Same Author

POETRY

THE LAND	*Heinemann*
KING'S DAUGHTER	*Hogarth Press*
COLLECTED POEMS	,, ,,
SOLITUDE	,, ,,

TRAVEL

PASSENGER TO TEHERAN	,, ,,
TWELVE DAYS	,, ,,

FICTION

THE EDWARDIANS	,, ,,
ALL PASSION SPENT	,, ,,
THE DARK ISLAND	,, ,,
FAMILY HISTORY	,, ,,
GRAND CANYON	*Michael Joseph*

BIOGRAPHY AND CRITICISM

PEPITA	*Hogarth Press*
ST. JOAN OF ARC	*Cobden Sanderson*
ANDREW MARVELL	*Faber & Faber*
APHRA BEHN	*Gerald Howe, Ltd.*

MISCELLANEOUS

SOME FLOWERS	*Cobden Sanderson*
COUNTRY NOTES	*Michael Joseph*
COUNTRY NOTES IN WARTIME	*Hogarth Press*

AVILA

V. SACKVILLE-WEST

THE EAGLE AND
THE DOVE

A Study in Contrasts

ST. TERESA OF AVILA
ST. THÉRÈSE OF LISIEUX

MICHAEL JOSEPH LTD
26 Bloomsbury Street, London, W.C.1

FIRST PUBLISHED IN 1943

*Set and printed in Great Britain by Unwin Brothers Ltd.,
at the Gresham Press, Woking, in Bembo type, eleven
point, leaded, and bound by James Burn*

Illustrations

AVILA
Frontispiece

A LETTER FROM ST. TERESA
facing p. 48

TOLEDO IN A STORM
facing p. 49

LES BUISSONNETS, LISIEUX
facing p. 144

ST. THÉRÈSE AT THE CONVENT OF LISIEUX
facing p. 145

★

Acknowledgements

As it has proved very difficult under war-time conditions to obtain necessary works of reference, particularly in foreign languages, I am more than ordinarily grateful to those who have come to my assistance, and would wish to thank especially the Right Reverend Lady Abbess of Stanbrook, Dame Laurentia McLachlan, O.S.B., and the Rev. R. H. J. Steuart, S.J., for loans from the libraries at Stanbrook Abbey and 114, Mount Street respectively. Without their generous help, this book could not now have been written.

I must thank also the Directors of the Metropolitan Museum, New York, for permission to reproduce the El Greco of Toledo in a storm.

Owing to the impossibility of communicating with France, I have been unable to ask permission from the Carmel of Lisieux for the reproduction of illustrations from *l'Histoire d'une âme*, but I trust that some day they may forgive me the unavoidable discourtesy.   V. S.-W.

To
TERESA-MARIA

"There is a God,—the most august of all conceivable truths."
CARDINAL NEWMAN

Saint Teresa of Avila

1515–1582

"I look down on the world as from a great height and care very little what people say or know about me. Our Lord has made my life to me now a kind of sleep, for almost always what I see seems to me to be seen as in a dream, nor have I any great sense either of pleasure or of pain."   ST. TERESA

I

THE saints in general are but little known to that non-Catholic branch of Christ's church which nevertheless and somewhat incongruously avows its belief in the Communion of Saints in its accepted creed. Half a dozen or so are vaguely familiar, but even these owe their popularity to some recognisable label: St. Anthony of Padua because he enjoys a reputation for finding lost objects; St. Francis of Assisi because he fed the birds; St. Joan of Arc because she heard voices, was burnt by the English, and saved France. We cherish also some saints to whom our insular interest attaches: St. Thomas à Beckett because he was murdered in Canterbury cathedral; St. Swithin because of his reputed influence on our climate; St. Columba because he landed in Scotland; St. Patrick because he landed in Ireland; St. George because he slew a dragon in Libya. Others have imprinted themselves on our imagination through the pictorial representations of the distressing trials they underwent: St. Sebastian because he was pierced by arrows; St. Catherine of Alexandria because she was broken on a wheel, oddly and unwittingly commemorated by us on the Fifth of November; St. Ursula because she was accompanied by eleven thousand virgins. None of these is a very profound or far-reaching reason for an acquaintance which would probably not stand up to any more extensive enquiry. Yet, whatever our beliefs may be, whether we spontaneously invoke St. Anthony when we have mislaid our keys or stalk with Puritan disapproval past the touching little shrines and statues which mean so much to a Catholic peasantry, there is a fascination to be found in the study of this life within life, this unique company, concealed but ardent, chronologically sparse but always similar in aim and often in actual detail of experience; this contradiction of all worldly values. Apparently unaccountable to many of us, to others even shocking in its suggestion of idolatry, there may yet come moments when as in any attempt to grasp a totally recondite subject (let us say Relativity), whose importance we know by repute but whose quest we have eschewed as being beyond our comprehension and certainly beyond any practical usefulness in the life we have to lead, a glimmer of understanding crosses our darkness, instantly gone again perhaps, but at least sufficient to show us that a truth is there and that our dismissal of it as meaningless, or meaningless to us, throws ourselves, not the subject, into a paltry light.

No mathematics or specialised knowledge are required for an appreciation of the saints. True, and especially in the case of the advanced mystics, we may find ourselves led sometimes into regions of theological technicalities which may appear but an otiose complication of a fundamentally simple proposition. In the matter of prayer alone, prayer, that vital means of access for the seeker after God, it may come as a surprise to discover the intricacies of systematised prayer; to discover how long a step there is between the simple, direct appeal and the instructed method of the advanced religious. There would seem to be something artificial about it; something too sophisticated; something which would interfere with the spontaneous approach of the soul to its Creator. The theologically uninformed asks himself whether he is to regard this as an unnecessary elaboration of the purely pious, worshipping, propitiating instinct, or as the advance always inevitable in the perfection of technique. Is he to regard it as comparable in poetry to the outpourings of the child or adolescent in raw verse, heartfelt but in the literary sense negligible, against the mature perfected achievement of the adult, preserving its sincerity under the control of craftsmanship? and as any form of stylised art may appear to the untrained eye, bearing no relation at all to the lower and easier function of "representation?" The refinements of the expert are always apt to provoke the annoyance of the amateur, but he will display a reasonable temper if he decides to consider with patience and tolerance the methods evolved by the informed. For, as we advance deeper into this unknown country it grows apparent that such charts and sign-posts, far from creating confusion where none should be, do indeed serve to clarify the way and become indispensable as the pilgrim trudges along the labyrinthine lanes of the soul. After all "The subject," as Teresa of Avila remarked, "is most difficult to understand without personal experience of such graces." It is indeed. We may agree further with St. Teresa when she observes that she wonders why God has not explained such difficult, occult subjects more fully, so that we could all understand Him. But in the main we are concerned with those things familiar, even though but spasmodically, to all: the intimations of another rule of life; the desire, faint perhaps, addled or abortive, to fulfil those intimations; a desire provoked, perhaps, only by some personal misfortune, some disaster which indicates that life is neither so secure nor so well-ordered as we should like to believe; a dissatisfaction with the prevailing code; the disquieting conviction that some solution of greater and infinitely more essential value has somehow eluded most people of the generations, past and present, of dwellers on this earth. It is not reasonable to suppose that a final apprehension of either the visible or the invisible world is necessarily to be reached only by means of our own five senses or even by the conjectures of our remarkable and vaunted brain. Such a supposition is as arrogant as it is limited. Even the most materially-minded amongst us know very well, in moments of fright and incertitude when an earthquake shudders the foundation of our pitiable structure, that our façade represents in no true way the answer lying somewhere else, behind it. What that answer may be, monosyllabic, brief, plain, and tremendous, we do not know. That it exists we cannot doubt. It is reasonable, on the other hand, to contend that if we admit the aim of mankind to be, on the whole, an aspiration towards an understanding of some Absolute, a discovery of some singleness in place of the fragmentary confusion which life offers, then we must also recognise that those who have sought, thoroughly, consistently, and exclusively the life of the spirit instead of the life of the world, demonstrate no more than an exaggerated exemplification of ourselves in those dim and rudimentary stirrings which the urgency of the visible world has so quickly suppressed.

Let us mention in parenthesis that on a less exalted but most perplexing plane the saints provide us with a series of problems not usually realised by the reader hitherto uninterested in such subjects. It would be frivolous to dwell at too great a length on the merely physical phenomena which so frequently accompany holiness both during life and after death; frivolous, unless turned into a special and separate study supported by much documentation and all the available scientific, medical, and theological evidence; but we may at least indulge ourselves to the extent of touching briefly on this exceedingly curious and unexplained aspect of the mystical life. It may be suggestive enough to make a short list of some peculiarities observed in hundreds of cases, leaving them without comment and resisting the temptation to supply a confusing number of instances. Such a list must be divided into two parts, the first concerned with the living body and the second with the dead. Among the living we shall find such surprising gifts as levitation, or the involuntary rising of the body into the air;* and the perhaps more notorious mystery of stigmatisation, or reproduction of the wounds of Christ, where the apparent physical injuries may be restricted to the hands and feet, but may also include the fifth wound, in the side; supplemented sometimes by the marks of the Crown of Thorns; and even in some rarer cases by the weals of the Flagellation and the bruises produced upon the shoulder by the weight of the Cross. (An autopsy held on St. Veronica Giuliani revealed a definite bending of the bone in the right shoulder, compatible with the carrying of such a heavy burden.) Stigmatisation, compared with levitation, is of rare occurrence, with only fifty or sixty cases worth considering on the evidence, the majority of them women. The earliest recorded case, with the possible exception of Blessed Dodo the Frisian, is that of St. Francis of Assisi, whose hands and feet "seemed pierced in the midst by nails, the heads of the nails appearing in the inner part of the hands and in the upper part of the feet and their points over against them, i.e. certain small pieces of flesh were seen like the ends of nails bent and driven back. . . . Moreover his right side, as if it had been pierced by a lance, was overlaid with a scar and often shed forth blood." This shedding of

* See infra, p. 53.

blood is a recognised incident in stigmatists, and usually takes place on Fridays. Less well-known, probably, is the manifestation called *incendium amoris*, where the temperature is raised beyond medical experience and the oppression of physical heat is such that the sufferer bathes himself with cold water in search of relief, or tears open his clothes, as St. Philip Neri who would walk with his chest uncovered through Rome even in the snow; and St. Mary Magdalen de' Pazzi was so distraught by this burning of love that she not only cut and tore her habit, but went out into the garden and tore up the plants, fanned her face with her veil, ran to the well, drank large quantities of water, poured it into her bosom, and behaved altogether in a manner indicative of the great oppression she felt. A certain Dominican nun, Maria Villani, aptly described as "a furnace of love," was said to give forth a sizzling sound like that of water falling on a sheet of red-hot iron whenever she drank; and the same hissing sound was observed whenever a cooling drench was poured over the Venerable Agnes of Jesus. A modern example, alive in 1923 though I cannot tell whether he is still living now, is found in a young Capuchin priest at Foggia, a stigmatist, whose temperature exceeds the register of any clinical thermometer and causes it to break.

So much for the living body. There is much more that could be said, and many strange happenings have been omitted, but the psychologically-minded will maintain that all such phenomena can, or could, be explained away if only we knew more about the influence of the mind upon the material tissues. They will maintain, with truth, that extreme ardour experienced by persons violently inspired is known to produce definite physical effects; that tremblings of the limbs, palpitations of the heart, sweats and shiverings, the pains of racked joints, even loss of sensibility and similar consequences of immoderate emotion are common to us all, though perhaps in lesser degree. Suspicions of hallucination and auto-suggestion will also be advanced. Let us turn therefore to the body after death, when the mind, presumably, can no longer be operative or in any way be held responsible.

Here we shall meet in the first place with the unaccountable problem of the incorruptibility of the body. It is established beyond all doubt that the remains of certain persons, even after the lapse of centuries, have not suffered the ordinary decomposition of mortal flesh. On this point there can be no argument at all. Nor do the conditions following upon death and burial appear to affect the matter; it is influenced neither by damp, nor quicklime, nor by delay in interment (and in many cases the reluctance of the devout to be separated from the object of their devotion has led to an abnormal procrastination, St. Bernardine of Siena for instance remaining unburied for twenty-six days, St. Angela Merici, Foundress of the Ursulines, for thirty days, St. Laurence Giustiniani for sixty-seven days), nor by such exceptional circumstances as those which occurred in the case of St. Josaphat, who was murdered and thrown into the river Dwina, retrieved after spending six days in the water, found then to be fresh and beautiful, and preserved his incorruption for many years afterwards. From the moment we begin to glance, however cursorily, at this subject, the more baffling does it become. For one thing, the marvel of incorruptibility is extremely erratic in its incidence, and would seem not necessarily to be associated with the degree of sanctity. Thus, neither St. Francis, St. Bernard, St. Dominic, St. Ignatius, St. Vincent Ferrer, St. Aloysius Gonzaga, St. Gabriel the Passionist, nor the subject of the second essay in this book, St. Thérèse of Lisieux, was spared the common lot of decay. On the other hand, this remarkable favour attends some of the most famous names in the Calendar, St. Charles Borromeo for example, dying in 1584, was found almost entire in 1880 despite a damp and leaky coffin; St. John of the Cross, dying in 1591, was still incorrupt in 1859. As for St. Teresa of Avila, we shall presently have occasion to record contemporary evidence on her preservation; and, coming down to more recent times, may note the case of the renowned Curé d'Ars, Jean-Baptiste Vianney, and that of St. Bernadette Soubirous of Lourdes, who, dying in 1879, was exhumed thirty years later and found to be without any trace of putrefaction. Erratic indeed; inconsistent, even whimsical, would appear the bestowal of this most strange dispensation. Sometimes it was inexplicably partial; St. Anthony, for instance, was allowed to disintegrate in the normal way, but his tongue remained "red, soft, and entire"— an object which aroused the veneration of Thérèse of Lisieux on a journey to Italy some six and a half centuries after his death.

Incorruptibility is not the only aberration from natural laws to be found in association with the dead body. Conspicuous among these other phenomena is the cadaveric rigidity (*rigor mortis*) which sets in a few hours after death and passes off within thirty-six hours, speaking approximately. Medical experience makes no exception for this law, but it is certain that the corpses of many holy persons have been known to remain supple throughout the period when rigidity was to be expected; we will quote only the case of St. Benedict Joseph Labre, who so entirely retained the flexibility and even the warmth of life for four days, that a surgeon examined his heart and lungs to make certain that he was really dead. Fragrance is yet another unexplained but well-authenticated attribute; the "odour of sanctity," in fact; a pleasant gift not always limited to the corpse, but shared also by those who quite certainly made no use of manufactured scents. "When we wanted the Reverend Mother," writes a nun of Blessed Maria of the Angels, "and could not find her in her cell, we used to track her by the fragrance she had left behind." It may be objected by the sceptic that such delightful scents existed only as an illusion in the nostrils of those concerned, though the accumulation of evidence weighs strongly against this theory; but what explanation can be found for another mystery, the exudation of an oily liquid from the incorrupt body and even, in rare cases, from the skeleton? St. Walburga, an Englishwoman, has exuded this peculiar unguent for over twelve hundred years.

These few indications, which could profitably be enlarged into a whole book, will at least suggest the very unusual region into which we are led by even a superficial examination of the chosen of God; though what bearing they may have upon the ultimate truths and virtues I should prefer another to say.

II

THERE is some irony in the reflection that Teresa of Avila, who may share with those few others the honour of being known at least by name to a possible ten per cent of the non-Catholic population of Great Britain, should have come down to us as the prototype of the hysterical, emotional woman writhing in a frenzy of morbid devotion at the foot of the Crucifix. Richard Crashaw is partly to be thanked for having familiarised her to us all, and partly to be reprehended for having presented her so indelibly in such a character. He wrote but half the truth, inspired by the coruscation of his own conversion, when he sent up "into the heaven of poetry this marvellous rocket of song,"

> O thou undaunted daughter of desires!
> By all thy dower of lights and fires;
> By all the eagle in thee, all the dove;
> By all thy lives and deaths of love;
> By thy large draughts of intellectual day,
> And by thy thirsts of love more large than they;
> By all thy brim-filled bowls of fierce desire,
> By thy last morning's draught of liquid fire,
> By the full Kingdom of that final kiss
> That seized thy parting soul, and sealed thee His . . .

Crashaw had evidently studied Teresa closely; he must have been acquainted with her autobiography and, from internal evidence, with some of her other writings also, for his two poems (despite their deplorable lapses) reveal a detailed following of her career; and perhaps he is not to be blamed if his English readers have seized upon the excitable note to the neglect of the other note he was discerning enough to introduce—the reference to her "large draughts of intellectual day." That strongly compressed phrase deserves to be pondered. It shoots a beam on to a very significant facet of this strange woman's make-up; it implicitly discountenances the misjudgment that she indulged almost voluptuously in the fits of possession that sometimes came upon her. Never, never, it cannot be over-emphasised, did any mystic more profoundly mistrust such seizures than this sane, vigorous, intelligent, humorous Spaniard, or lose fewer opportunities of warning other people against them.

III

TERESA DE CEPEDA DÁVILA Y AHUMADA* was born at Avila in the province of Old Castile at dawn on March 28th, 1515. Avila is an ancient and, to our minds, startlingly picturesque city entirely surrounded by massive walls fortified by nearly a hundred circular and crenelated towers, and pierced at intervals by gates giving admission to the narrow streets. Standing on the flat table of a ridge that rises abruptly from rocky bluffs, its altitude of nearly four thousand feet and its unprotected exposure to the winds that tear straight off the snows of the Sierra de Malagon, the Sierra de Avila, and the Paramera de Avila render its climate harsh in the extreme. This is central Spain, no country of sunny patios, fountains, and orange-blossom, but a dour and ascetic land where the men go wrapped in cloaks, a corner thrown across the shoulder, so muffled that, with the hat pulled well down over the eyes, the fine and bony features are almost hidden; a land where honour is of fierce importance, the quarrel quick and mortal. It is a common and conventional error to regard all Spain as the gay land of romance and song. Excessive and without compassion, the spirit of El Greco's Toledo in its lurid storm comes closer in truth to the tortured intemperance of a fanatical people. Spain, in some aspects, is terrible, not soft, not pretty. Castile, not only geologically, is made of granite. Northern though it is, there are no mists here, no softening of the naked ashen plains, but a clear light relentlessly discouraging dreams and fallacies, and leaving only the realistic truth as these people see it. Their imagination runs along the same stern lines—the polished lance-like imagination of an honourable chivalry. Don Quixote rides these plains on a gaunt horse. He may be an idealist, but realism always keeps him company. It is as impossible to lose the consciousness of strife in this country where a gritty dust stings the eyes in winter or a shadowless sun burns the hands on the reins in summer, as to remain without the enlargement of the spirit begotten

* The Spanish use of surnames is apt to cause some confusion. A woman keeps her own surname, adding it on to that of her husband, thus Teresa's mother, Beatriz Dávila y Ahumada, on marrying Alonso de Cepeda, Teresa's father, becomes Beatriz de Cepeda Dávila y Ahumada. In present days it is customary for the children to take the surnames of both parents, but in Teresa's day they could adopt the surname of either their father or their mother, irrespective of their own sex. Thus Teresa called herself Ahumada after her mother, though her sister Maria called herself Cepeda after their father.

of all desolate places. Practical ability and mysticism were not incompatible attributes in the children of this soil where Avila itself was proverbially said to be made of stones and saints.

Inside the city walls, poverty was visible in the many miserable beggars, for much of the old activity had departed since the suppression of the Jews and the expulsion of the Moors who, with their Arab luxury and colour, had done something to soften the austerity of granite Spain. A reaction had set in amongst the indigenous families of Castile, a reaction against that alien civilisation: corrupted for a time, they had now reverted to type and little evidence of the Arab element remained save in the presence of a few Moorish slaves moving noiselessly about the staircases of the rough palaces. Ascetism not indulgence was again the note, an asceticism compounded of soldierly honour and religious intensity, a mixture of sobriety and excess, severity and pride. There was the background of high deeds, celebrated in romance, a romance dressed not in silks and velvets but in leather and chain-mail. There were stone floors and thick walls, all gray; and between the battlements the views opened over the gray plains where a convoy of waggons slowly crawled or a messenger rode swathed and huddled on his mule. Life in Avila was closely self-contained; shepherds and goatherds from the hills might come in to market, and companies of professional mountebanks tumble for a few coppers inside the gates; but little truck was held even with other cities, Segovia or Salamanca, not so very far away. Transport was difficult, travel dangerous, and there was little reason for the inhabitants to go much beyond their walls except in search of adventure such as took their sons away on the supreme adventure of the new Spain in the new continent overseas.

Racial pride was extreme, not only on account of the native arrogance of the Castilians, but also on the triple account of the Moorish infiltration, the hated Jews, and the damning Inquisition. For a Spaniard to hold his head high, it was necessary to boast of impeccably limpid blood, *limpia sangre*; the purity or *limpieza* which meant total freedom from all Jewish or Mohammedan connexions, and freedom also from descent from anybody once condemned by the Inquisition; a mishap which could not be disguised, for the guilty were forced to wear a yellow robe marked with the cross of St. Andrew. The Cepeda were fortunately secure in this respect, and no taint attached to Alonso de

Cepeda, his two wives, or his twelve children. They could all enjoy the hidalgo's privilege of *tratamiento* which conferred the prefix of Don or Doña, very superfluous in the case of Teresa who always entered into a rage of indignation when any well-meaning person addressed her by a title. The Cepeda were beyond suspicion in their palace near the ramparts which happened to stand in the old deserted Jewish quarter. Its surroundings must thus have been very derelict indeed, leaving it as a fortress-abode of life in the midst of silence. The sedulous Jews, traders and manufacturers, workers in cloth and carpets and metals, who had once animated the city with their industry, had fled, eleven thousand of them, nearly half the total population, twenty-three years earlier, a tide rapidly receding from the Cepeda walls that loomed above the flotsam and jetsam of the abandoned streets. Here Teresa was born and brought up, taking as her companion for choice her brother Rodrigo, four years her senior, a little boy of inflamed imagination whose readings and pastimes she shared. There were no Moorish slaves in the Cepeda palace; Don Alonso, a humane man, disapproved of slaves, so the household was strictly and entirely Spanish.

The children's mother, Beatriz de Ahumada, married Don Alonso as his second wife at the age of fourteen, bore him nine children, and faded out of life when she was thirty-three. Her story must be very similar to that of multitudes of other Spanish girls, practically incarcerated within their husbands' domain. Many people, many women, have lived and died and silence has closed over them, lost without trace. But as Thérèse Martin, more than three hundred years later, was to switch the little torch of her pen on to the simple annals of a middle-class home in Lisieux, so did Teresa in Avila illuminate the gloomy corners of a palace sick-room where her mother lay, looking older than her years. She was of great beauty, according to her daughter, but took no trouble to exploit it; too ill, poor lady, for any such vanity, her one pleasure consisted in reading romantic tales of which her husband did not approve. Teresa thought that although this recreation did her mother little harm, for she never wasted time over it, it was a pity she left her children full liberty to read as much as they pleased, in order to keep them occupied and to prevent them from going astray in other ways; and it is indeed intelligible to the harshest judgment that a sick woman with a scatter of high-spirited

B

children to control would welcome any method of keeping them quiet. Suitably, she remains always in a shadowy background, her very name, Ahumada, swirling a veil of smoke round her, as the smoke had poured from the armorial bearings of her family, a burning tower defended to the last against the Moors. There were two boys of the first marriage and seven boys of her own to come round her bed and say their prayers, besides one girl of the first marriage and two of her own, but of these two only Teresa could really take her place among her brothers, for the other little girl, Juana, was the baby of the whole family.

Teresa and Rodrigo were the pair who gave their mother the greatest anxiety; they had inherited her taste for reading and they also listened greedily to the stories she told them, but the mixture proved too strong for their small heads. Tales of adventure and tales of martyr-dom combined in a vision of such glamour that it must instantly be translated into action. It was secretly arranged between them that they must run away to Africa, for they had of course heard much of the Moors as the enemies of Spain and the true religion. Once arrived in Africa, they would manage to get themselves beheaded, taking a short-cut, in fact, to Heaven. They had read the lives of the saints together, and were much attracted by the idea of martyrdom, though, as Teresa candidly admits, they were unconscious of any particular love for God and merely wanted to attain the great joys they understood were reserved for them in the after-life. To their credit, the thought of their father and mother did trouble them a little; it was their chief difficulty, *el mayor embarazo*. But they had worked themselves into a state of excitement where nothing could be allowed to stand in the way; they had discovered from their reading that not only pain but bliss was everlasting, and hypnotised them-selves into this belief by constantly repeating, "For ever, ever, ever," *para siempre, siempre, siempre!* From Teresa's account, one must sup-pose that they trotted about the palace, seriously muttering these words. It was their intention to walk to Africa, begging alms on the way, but, since they were not devoid of the Castilian practical good sense, noticeable in Teresa throughout her life, they did take the precaution to lay in a secret stock of dried raisins for the opening stages of their journey.

They started off through the Adaja gate, crossing the bridge in the direction of Salamanca. Teresa was seven, and Rodrigo eleven. They must inevitably have heard a great deal about the dangers of the road in everyday talk at home, but such things do not mean very much to children; they are merely words with no visual accompaniment, and at best provide only an exciting supplement to the adventures of their heroes in poetry and fiction. It is quite sufficient to tell a child that if it runs away, it will be stolen by gipsies to make this peril immediately appear the most desirable fate that could befall it. Though Teresa believed in retrospect that she knew what beheading meant and would have had the required courage, one may be permitted to doubt it. Fortunately, the enterprise did not carry them very far; they were soon missed at home and servants were sent running up and down the streets in search of them, but meanwhile they had scarcely gained the open country when they met their uncle Francisco who naturally took the culprits straight back to their mother. Teresa states that she was always very calm and full of good sense, but on this occasion she did imagine that her children had fallen down a well. Faced by her reproaches, Rodrigo failed in all the traditions of chivalry, laying the blame on "the little one," *la niña*, who, he said, had wanted to see God and had wanted to die as quickly as possible in order to do so.

This treachery on Rodrigo's part does not seem to have affected their alliance, for, thwarted in one project, they are next to be found playing together at hermits in their father's garden. There were plenty of stones lying about on that rocky soil, but alas the 'caves' tumbled in as soon as they had built them, for they were not strong enough to lift the bigger stones which might have kept the construction in place. But they had other resources to pass the time. There were books in the house; tinder to throw on the flames of their imagination. "So completely was I mastered by this passion," Teresa says, "that I thought I could never be happy without a book." It annoyed their father so much that they had to be careful he never saw them. Don Alonso had a library of his own, but with one or two exceptions, (some poetry, and *La Gran Conquista de Ultramar*,) his shelves were filled with volumes of a most serious character, for example Cicero's *De officiis*, Boethius' *De Consolatione philosophiae*, Seneca's *Proverbs*, the devotional verses of Perez de Guzman, and Juan Padilla's *Retablo de la vida de Cristo*. With the aid of these books Don Alonso himself had taught Teresa to read—which suggests an unusual degree of enlightenment on his part in days when it was by no means considered necessary for a daughter of the nobility to master the art either of reading or of writing—not foreseeing that the acquirement would immediately send her in quest of more attractive matter. This she found in her mother's room, where all the lighter literature had migrated, literature which was not only heroic and gallant in tone, but also extremely coarse and outspoken. She says she spent many hours of the day and night hidden from her father (presumably the mother who had given her this taste was dead by then, for she died when Teresa was about thirteen), and she blames a great many of her shortcomings on this frivolous occupation. She and Rodrigo could think of nothing but honour and heroism, knights and giants and distressed ladies, defeated evil and conquering virtue; they even collaborated in composing a story of their own, modelled on these lines. One would give much to read it, but the manuscript is lost.

IV

TERESA may have been right in thinking that this feast of romance had a deleterious effect on her character, but perhaps the natural inclinations of her age were equally responsible, for she entered now upon a stage when she thought only of amusing herself as best she could within the very severe limitations imposed upon every Spanish girl. In this, as in many other things, how markedly she differed from her little namesake of Lisieux, who at a similar age was struggling and scheming and pleading and weeping to get herself into Carmel!

It is somewhat difficult to see on what ground Teresa criticises herself so harshly, for however dashing her tendencies she can have had but little opportunity to indulge them. It is not even likely that, having no mother but only an older sister to keep an eye on her, she over-stepped the code in a house with a father vigilant in the background and nine brothers coming in and out. The reputation of any woman, whether married or unmarried, was an intensely serious matter in which death could very quickly become involved; too open a familiarity, or what might be interpreted as such, must like a magnet persuade the dagger from the sheath, nor might the closest ties of friendship or even kinship between men stand in the way for one instant when there was any question of avenging an insult to their women. Daughter, sister, cousin, wife, all is one. It is remarkable that this excessive and protective jealousy should be found in Spain to a far greater degree than in any other European country, greater even than in Italy where nevertheless the blood is equally inflammable and *crimes passionels* of common occurrence. In Spain the defence of the code of honour had developed into a regular system. Not only must an affront (*agravio*) be instantly avenged, but a woman annoyed in the street had the right to demand protection from any man, even a stranger. This arrangement provided an absurd refinement, namely, that if the woman happened to be in disguise for her own reasons she could thus get herself defended against the pursuit of an enraged husband or father while she herself made good her escape. It is one of the functions of art to exaggerate its chosen subject, and doubtless the cloak-and-sword dramatists made the most of their material, but at least there was enough residue of fact for their plays to make sense to the audience. The kernel of actuality was there, to be found behind the iron window-bars of every home.

Spain had never adopted from the Moors the total seclusion of her women, but she had done the nearest she could get to it. The restraint may have been a necessary one to impose on a passionate race, and its consequences were of course heightened to an extreme degree by the exclusive nature of the Spaniards. It is not pride alone which closes a Spanish house to strangers; it is an inherent absence of the spirit of hospitality; not even superficially, within his own home, is the Spaniard welcoming or gregarious. He keeps his social contacts for the club or the café, but the home is for his family and his women, and seldom indeed will even his closest outside friend be invited to share a meal within that shut circle. But, as might recently be observed in America, prohibition has its dangers. Lively youth will not be wholly repressed, and the more hazardous the game the greater its attraction. Rigid though Spanish morality might be, there was still an unavowed respect for the daring young man who could circumvent it, and an amused esteem for the young woman who, without going too far, could provoke him into a desire to do so. Teresa de Ahumada was such a young woman. She liked people;

she was warmly affectionate, and wanted her affection returned; she had no hesitation in raising a clamour when she thought she was not getting as much as she gave, ("I love you dearly; I was keenly hurt at not meeting such love and simplicity from you";) she was responsive when she met with appreciation, ("whenever I found any-one well-disposed towards myself, and I liked him, I used to have such an affection for him as compelled me always to remember and think of him";) she loved conversation, and all her life was reputed a brilliant and voluble talker, ("I always had the defect of making myself understood only with a torrent of words";) she loved gaiety, which in her view was "necessary to render life bearable;" she was full of humour, sometimes rather malicious; her letters prove it. From many little indications that she inadvertently lets slip,—inadvertently, for in her extreme and often exasperating humility she would never consciously write anything a later reader might piece together to her credit—she emerges as a truly charming woman, a woman one would like to know. She was warm through and through. Generous, "if I were possessed of a jewel or any other thing that gave me great pleasure, and it came to my knowledge that a person whom I loved more than myself and whose satisfaction I preferred to my own, wished to have it, it would give me great pleasure to deprive myself of it, because I would give all I possessed to please that person;" impulsive; humanly fallible too, "the Devil sends so offensive a spirit of bad temper that I think I could eat people up;" ardent, "when I desire anything I am accustomed naturally to desire it with some vehemence;" grateful; "I see that in my case gratitude has nothing to do with holiness; it must be in my nature, for anyone who gave me so much as a sardine could obtain anything from me" (me subornaran). She possessed furthermore the intellectual's quality of curiosity; she wishes she knew "the properties of things; I am amused and interested by them." There is no need for imagina-tive reconstruction to discover that she possessed all the delightful attributes which arouse an instant interest, sympathy, and response in widely differing types of people, whether the boyish cousins who frequented her home, or the nuns at the convent of the Encarnacion who made much of her "for our Lord had given me the grace to please everyone, wherever I might be," or so grave and emaciated a saint as Pedro de Alcantara who she said "seemed made of roots of trees, more than anything else." Throughout her life she had innumerable friends, whom she managed, scolded, teased, cajoled, coerced, mothered, and kept always in close devotion however exacting she might be, simply because apart from her bewildering qualities of holiness she possessed also the human quality of a genius for friendship. She could, it is clear, get on with anybody; at the least, she amused and stimulated; and those who were admitted to a fuller knowledge of that rich nature never escaped from her toils nor wished to.

For the moment the higher side of her nature was unrevealed. Nothing was apparent except the exterior charm of a loving and loveable girl, lively, intelligent, sociable and enterprising, with the additional advantage of being good-looking and making the most of it. "I began to make much of dress, to wish to please others by my appearance. I took pains with my hands and hair, used perfumes and all vanities within my reach, and they were many, for I was very much given to them." She had evidently not taken to heart the words of St. Jerome about "those who paint their cheeks with rouge and their eyelids with antimony; whose plastered faces, too white for human beings, look like idols, and if in a moment of forget-fulness they shed a tear it makes a furrow where it rolls down the painted cheek; they who load their heads with other people's hair and enamel a lost youth upon the wrinkles of age." Nevertheless, Teresa's vanity had its good side. Her fastidiousness, and a real mania for cleanliness in every respect, come as a slight surprise considering the century in which she lived; it was a subject on which she was later perpetually bothering her Prioresses and even her friends. Although in accordance with her vow of poverty as a nun she wore nothing but an old patched habit, she was always very particular that all her garments should be clean; and so noticeable was this idiosyncracy that her contemporary biographer remarks, unconsciously throwing a light on his own times, "her coifs and tunics never smelt of sweat or any other unpleasant smell, like those of other people." One is reminded of St. Christina the Astonishing who, like Teresa, paid no attention to the appearance of her habit which consisted of no more than rags held together by twigs, but who so much disliked the smell of human bodies that she thought nothing of climbing trees, flinging herself into mill-races, or crawling into

ovens to escape the offending odour, and during her own requiem
Mass flew from her coffin up to the roof, away from the congregation,
and perched there on the rafters until the priest made her come
down again.

For the outward semblance of Teresa there exists a detailed description compiled by a Jesuit friar who had known her personally and
furthermore in his anxiety to get his facts right had consulted many
people intimately acquainted with her. From a preconception, and
misconception, we might imagine her to be tall, forbidding; aquiline,
even haggard; bony, even cadaverous; impressive, but uncomely;
momentous, but unapproachable. Not at all. She was somewhat
plump (*abultada*, or bulky), with a white skin and a good deal of
colour; curly black hair; thick reddish eyebrows, almost straight;
round black eyes, somewhat prominent (*papujados*, or swollen), very
vivacious and laughing, so that when she laughed, everybody laughed,
yet they could be very grave when she wanted to express gravity.
Her nose was straight with a rounded and slightly drooping tip, the
nostrils small and arched; her mouth neither small nor large, with a
thin straight upper lip but the lower lip thick and rather drooping;
good teeth; a broad, short neck, rather thick in front. Three little
moles added to the piquancy of her face: one halfway down her nose,
one between her nose and her mouth, and one just beneath her mouth.
Her hands were pretty and small (*muy lindas aunque pequeñas*); her
feet were small too, and after her death were seen to be transparent
as mother-of-pearl; a gentleman had once caught sight of them and
complimented Teresa, who without a blush replied, "Have a good
look, *caballero*, for this is the last time you will see them." It is clear
from all this that she was what we should call a typically Spanish
woman. We may add, that judging by her full-length portrait, and
also by the probability indicated by her nationality, she was short
and somewhat stocky of build. How did she dress as a girl? at least
one of her dresses has been described by an old nun who remembered
it: it was orange, trimmed with black velvet braid.

It is evident that her natural vanity never wholly deserted her, for
when in later years Fray Juan de la Miseria painted her portrait she said
"May God forgive you, Fray Juan! what I have had to suffer at your
hands, and after all to paint me ugly and blear-eyed!" (*fea y legañosa*).

Teresa, later in life, naturally held the most orthodox views about the position of women, views which in any case would have proceeded from her profession, but which also reflect the attitude of her age and nation: a married woman, she says, dare not speak of her most serious maladies and poignant trials lest she annoy her husband, if he is sad, she too must appear unhappy; if he is merry, although she may be feeling far from cheerful she must appear light-hearted also; and from an unlawful attachment may God deliver us! It is a perfect hell, never to be mentioned; we must never remember that it exists, nor even hear it named either in jest or earnest. But Teresa at fourteen was unregenerate. She would be cautious, certainly, for she greatly feared disgrace and her own nature would prevent her from failing in the honour of the world, but within those limits she would enjoy life; and, she adds, "I was very adroit in doing anything that was wrong." The picture she draws is extremely vivid: a band of young cousins, boys, all round about her own age, some a little older, who were always with her and had a great affection for her. It was she who kept the conversation alive in everything that gave them pleasure, their loves and their follies; and it is indicated that her sister Maria, a quiet and sober young woman, much older than herself, stood quite outside this gay circle with no influence upon Teresa. The influence came, instead, from one of the cousins, a girl whom Teresa's mother had so greatly mistrusted that she had taken great pains to keep her away; but, owing to the kinship and the many reasons for her coming, she could not actually be forbidden the house. Don Alonso and Maria, equally distressed by this friendship, were likewise handicapped, and Teresa continued to enjoy the gossip, the recital of affairs and vanities, and, clearly, profited by the part of go-between that this unclean and parasitical tempter was willing to play. The servants, too, she found "ready enough for all evil." This is where it becomes difficult to determine what Teresa really did. It is clear that she blames herself bitterly for something; she uses strong words, "mortal sin," "blinded by passion;" and insists that the fear of God had utterly departed from her though the fear of dishonour remained, a torment in all she did. However scrupulous her conscience in retrospect, this is scarcely the language she would have used, even allowing for the excessive rigour of the Spanish code, even allowing for the degree of sanctity she had attained by the time she wrote this account, in referring to some boy-and-girl cousinly flirtation or to a temporary relish for the salacious conversation of older girls. Whatever her apologists may say, for three months something very dark was taking place in Teresa's life; something so dark according to her views that she never brought herself to be explicit on paper. It concerns the girl cousin and "another who was given to the same kind of pastimes" (*otra que tenia la misma manera de pasatiempos*). It is to be noted that this "other," so ambiguous in English, appears in the feminine in the Spanish original; and, since few things are more distasteful than veiled hints, it may also be outspokenly noted that in her own country the name of Teresa has been associated with that of Sappho. The authority (Vicente de la Fuente) who records this suspicion attaching to her reputation adds rather superfluously that no closer comparison with the lascivious, obscene, and unbridled loves of Sappho should be drawn than between the honeycombs of the bee and the wasp. Nobody in their senses or with any knowledge of this most misunderstood aspect of natural psychology would dream of comparing the organised orgies of Lesbos with the rudimentary experimental dabblings of adolescent girls, sciolists whose tentative essays may wither with maturity. The point is in any case perhaps not of very much interest, except in so far as every point concerning so complex a character and so truly extraordinary a make-up is of interest as possibly throwing a little extra light on subsequent behaviour. Above all, it is not introduced here in any spirit of scandalous disrespect to a wise woman and a great saint. But it may well supply the clue to this mysterious and tormented chapter in her autobiography, taken in conjunction with a further remark, to the effect that she had never constrained any man to like her, the Lord keeping her from it, but that had He abandoned her she might well have done wrong in this, *as she did in other things.* In yet another passage she states that she was afraid of marriage.

Her account is both confused and confusing. After bringing these vague but forcible accusations against herself, and saying that when she thought nobody would ever know she ventured upon many things neither honourable nor pleasing to God, she ends up by saying that, the occasion of sin being present and danger at hand, she exposed it all to her father and brothers. Yet, again, she says that so deep was her dissembling and so excessive her father's love for her, that he never would believe her to be so wicked as she was, and she never fell into disgrace with him. Must this be taken to mean that she had not after all been entirely open with him? or that he had discountenanced a confession in which he feared to believe? Whatever the explanation, Don Alonso took the practical step of putting her into a convent. Here, once more, she contradicts herself, for, after saying that she had told all to her father and brothers, she states that her relegation to the convent was done with the utmost concealment of the true reason, known only to herself and one of her kindred. Teresa's memory was always bad; she was constantly apologising for it, and also for the fact that she never had time to read over what she had written, but such apologies are scarcely valid in this instance where the contradiction occurs within a few lines of the document. The whole passage, even under the most honest examination, must remain a mystery.

V

TERESA at this stage had no desire whatsoever for the religious life. As a sixteenth-century Spaniard and a Catholic she could not fail to venerate God, with a corresponding dread of the Devil and a very vivid mental picture of Hell, but it cannot be emphasised too strongly that she was no vocational nun. Her seven-year-old fancy for martyrdom had originated in a search for adventure and a hankering after the fulfilment of promises, not clearly understood, but advertised as being held in reserve in heaven. Her sixteen-year-old entry into the Augustinian convent of Santa Maria de Gracia was imposed upon her from the outside, not by her own insistence or volition. Hers is a very strange case. One is tempted to say that she not only became the inmate of a cloister by convention, but became a saint by accident. True, it might be an accident ordained by God, a mysterious and fortuitous choice of instrument; for certainly neither in her early years nor in her visible nature did any indication exist of a tendency towards so high a calling. The very thought of becoming a nun filled her with repugnance. She says so quite frankly and with her usual energy. "I was most hostile to being a nun," (*estaba enemigisma de ser monja*). Yet not only did she become a nun, but also, after the lapse of many years spent in monastic obscurity and seclusion, one of

the most energetic reformers with new foundations of the Unmiti-
gated Rule to her credit all over Spain.

Meanwhile she was not even a postulant, but merely a pupil, and,
after the first week, not unhappy. She much enjoyed the conversation
of the young nun in charge of the secular children, and the evil
cousinly influence began to be rooted out. By the end of her eighteen
months' stay in that convent she was beginning to consider the possibility of embracing the monastic life, though determined it should
not be at Santa Maria de Gracia, if at all, but in the Carmelite convent
of the Encarnacion where a great friend of hers was already professed.
But although these good thoughts came to her from time to time,
they very soon left her again and she could not persuade herself to
any decision.

It may seem strange, considering her aversion, that she should
have entertained the thought for more than a moment, but, given
her objection to marriage, there was really no other alternative.
Besides this factor, which she does not mention—it was perhaps too
obvious to her mind—there was another factor which she mentions
strongly. It was fear. She describes her motive with absolute candour,
taking no pains to disguise the remarkable lack of enthusiasm with
which she gradually decided on the step. She began, she says, to be
afraid that if she were to die she would go to Hell; and although
she still could not bend her will to be a nun, she resolved to force
herself into it, little by little, because she saw that the religious state
was safest (*mas siguro*) and best. The abandonment of self to love,
the love of Christ, the anguished adoration of the suffering Saviour,
the ecstasy of surrender to the heavenly Bridegroom, such as we
find in Thérèse of Lisieux, is far more intelligible even to those who
somewhat cynically attribute it to a psychological, neuropathic
cause from which sex, however innocently and unawaredly, is not
absent. No such explanation can be advanced in the case of Teresa
of Avila. There is even one curious phrase embedded in her autobiography in which she refers to her "hatred of our Lord, which I
made so public." Even allowing for her habitual exaggeration in
self-accusation, this is going far indeed. So it was "more influenced
by servile fear than by love" that for three months she argued with
herself, persuading herself that the trials of living as a nun could
not be greater than those of Purgatory, whereas she, personally, had

well deserved to be in Hell. It would not be much, she argued, to spend the rest of her life as though she were in Purgatory and then go straight to Heaven, which was what she desired. The words scarcely make sense to our ears, nor is it easy to understand a terror so extreme that she preferred to do violence to all her own inclinations and to sacrifice a life which offered many attractions, sooner than run the risk of meeting that remote but, to her, very concrete fate. It is, indeed, impossible to understand it at all, unless we can succeed in shaping our mind to the very contours of Teresa's own, and in grasping not only with our minds but with our emotions the appalling reality of her conceptions. It is all the more difficult, given our knowledge of Teresa as an active, practical woman; an organiser and administrator full of determination and decision, to whom no detail was too small, no enterprise too intimidating; a woman shrewd and, in her dealings with the world, of great firmness and no illusions. Even in her attitude towards her own extraordinary experiences she gives reiterated proof of the utmost caution, dreading delusion no less than she dreaded Satan himself, dreading exaggeration, endeavouring to conceal her sudden trances from others, unwilling, resentful, yet all the time convinced of the terrible truth.

The exact nature of her visions must remain unexplained, though she herself went to the most scrupulous pains to explain it. They would come upon her at the most unexpected and inconvenient moments, when she was busy with other things and had no intention either of being rapt away into Heaven or bodily shaken by the possession of satanic power. They would come upon her when her mind was quite otherwise occupied, and were physically shattering in their effects. They embarrassed her exceedingly, so great was her fear that those who happened to be with her should perceive something to be the matter and should find out what it really was. Often she went away to hide herself from view; and sometimes she would not even dare to ask for holy water when devils were present although she knew it to be the sovereign remedy. This shrinking, this desire for secrecy and privacy, is far removed from the exhibitionism of the hysteric determined to be interesting at any cost.

She could not help herself, and, since she was given to the most meticulous accuracy in all matters, even to a painful parenthetical extent, for ever checking, qualifying, apologising, correcting, modify-

ing, it may be taken that she set down nothing she did not really believe. For one thing, her natural and searching honesty apart, she would have been afraid to do so; she was writing by the specific order of her confessor and for his eye alone; indeed, she enjoins secrecy upon him, almost as though she were speaking under the seal of the confessional: he may publish the recital of her sins as an advertisement to others, that they may not think her better than she is, but she will give him no leave to publish the rest, nor, if it be shown to anyone, will she consent to the name of the author being revealed. On the whole, if what she writes is not correct, let him destroy it. At best, it is very difficult for her to write at all, for she is living in a very poor house and has many things to do; her writing hinders her from spinning; she can write only little at a time and wishes she had more leisure, for when a writer is in the mood (or, as she puts it, when our Lord gives the spirit) it is easier and better done; it is then as with a person working embroidery with the pattern before her, but when the spirit is wanting, i.e. when inspiration is lacking, there is no more meaning in words than in gibberish.*
No one understood better than St. Teresa this inconvenient peculiarity of the artist, and her experiences in this matter might profitably be included in any study on the subject of inspiration. "I see clearly that it is not I who speak, nor is it I who with her understanding has arranged it; and afterwards I do not know how I came to speak so accurately. It has often happened to me thus."

To return. That Teresa's beliefs should seen to us incredible is beside the point. That she was no ignorant peasant, ready to be scared by any tale of superstition, but a woman of breeding and some culture, accustomed to the society of learned men, is irrelevant also, since her associates naturally shared her own convictions. The point is that she held those beliefs as a daughter of her country and her century. She held them to such an extent that they drove her step by step into a life she did not desire. She literally frightened herself into a convent; it was "the safest," the most secure. The intimations of love were there too, but they were very weak and spasmodic; their full revelation was to come much later. The fear from which

---

* The word she uses is *algaravia*, meaning literally the Arabic tongue; but popularly gabble or jargon to the Spaniards who had heard so much Arabic from the Moors.

she suffered, and its concreteness, can be realised only through her own descriptions, explain them as we may. The Devil, his personal appearance, his abode, and his wiles were very real to her; she speaks of his intrigues as of a mischievous person she might have known in the world, almost in a matter-of-fact, taken-for-granted way; his mischief is to do all in his power to steal souls from God, with so much subtlety and ingenuity and disguise that it is necessary to be continually on guard; had she been acquainted with the word and art of camouflage she, who liked realistic similes, would certainly have used it in illustration of his designs. The most innocent and even elevated symptoms of grace must be suspect lest they proceed from the evil realms. He works like a file, secretly and silently wearing its way; he would turn Hell upside down a thousand times to make us think ourselves better than we are. You think you have attained humility and other virtues? oh no, they are sham virtues springing from the evil root, accompanied by a vainglory never found in those of divine origin. He can affect you even by means of things so trivial that you would laugh at them at any other time; he can make the soul stumble over anything he likes, lays it in fetters, makes it lose all control over itself and all power of thinking of anything but the absurdities he puts before it. Then, the devils make a ball of the soul (*jugando a la pelota*), and it is unable to escape out of their hands. And as for his personal appearance, let Teresa continue to speak for herself: she was once in an oratory when Satan in an abominable shape appeared at her left hand. She looked at his mouth in particular because he was speaking to her, and it was frightful (*espantable*). A huge flame seemed to issue out of his body, perfectly bright, without any shadow. He spoke to her in a fearful way, saying that although she had escaped out of his hands he would yet lay hold of her again. In great terror she made the sign of the cross, when the form vanished, only to reappear instantly. Not knowing what to do, she took some holy water and threw it in the direction of the figure which then vanished without return.

Nor was this all. On another occasion she saw "a frightful little negro" gnashing his teeth in despair at losing what he attempted to seize. Teresa, who was meanwhile in great pain and violently shaken in the body, arms, and head, derided him and had no fear; her only fear was lest those who were with her should notice and be afraid.

She must have been a disquieting housemate and companion, for these perturbations came upon her without the slightest warning. At last, as her pain could not be relieved, she told them that if they would not laugh at her she would ask for some holy water. They brought it, and with her own hand she threw some in the direction of the negro, who fled in a moment and all her sufferings with him, except that she was tired and felt as though she had been beaten with many blows. Holy water, to her thinking, was of greater efficacy even than the sign of the cross, which dismissed evil spirits but did not preclude their return; holy water, however, sent them away for good. Upon her own soul it had a most refreshing effect, and this was no fancy, for she had watched it very carefully, and several times had put it to the test. Undoubtedly there was a great difference between holy water and water that had never been blessed.

By the same means she abolished Satan who had put himself on her open Breviary, to prevent her finishing her prayers; this time she saw also some souls coming out of Purgatory, and thought that Satan must have been trying to hinder their deliverance. Another time she saw a great fight between evil spirits and angels; and yet again a great multitude of evil spirits all round her, from whom she was preserved by an enveloping light. She learned, however, that after holy water there was nothing the Devil disliked so much as contempt, and that every time she was able to despise these terrors their force lessened and the soul gained corresponding power. To this end, she sometimes addressed him as "Goose."

Sometimes he appeared multiplied, as when she saw a dead body in a winding sheet, tossed to and fro by devils who also dragged it about with great hooks. She was so frightened as to be almost out of her senses at the sight and it required no slight courage on her part not to betray her distress. Another time she saw two devils with their horns fitted round the throat of a priest bearing the Host. She was pleased, however, when one day she saw a devil quite near her in a great rage, tearing to pieces some paper which he had in his hands, for then she knew that her prayer for the repentance of a certain person had been granted. It was less pleasing when the Devil pushed her with such violence that she struck her head and body against the wall.

And if the Devil, or his envoys, could manifest themselves with such precision, the same might be said of the place from whence they came. Teresa's vision of Hell was topographical in its exactitude. She was one day in prayer when she found herself, without knowing how, plunged apparently into the internal regions. The entrance was by a long, narrow pass (callejon) like a furnace, very low and dark and close; the ground saturated with water and mud, exceedingly foul, sending forth pestilential odours and covered with loathsome vermin. At the end was a hollow place in the wall like a cupboard, and in that she saw herself confined. She could neither sit nor lie down, there was no room; there was no light, only thick darkness. But all that was pleasant to behold in comparison with what she felt while she was there. She had read, she said, of the diverse tortures and how the devils tore the flesh with red-hot pincers, but all this was a wholly different matter. She is anxious, as always, to emphasise that her vision is real, original, and actual, not subjectively derived from anything she has heard or read, and moreover she explains in another place that her deliberate imagination was so sluggish, she never could picture even our Lord's humanity, however hard she might labour. Her corporeal body, indeed, was racked by unendurable sufferings—and she knew something of physical pain; her own physicians had told her that the contraction of her sinews when she was paralysed was the greatest that could be borne—but even this was nothing to the spiritual torment she endured. She could not see how to describe it, save by saying that she felt a fire in her soul. It was not even as though her soul were being torn from her body, for that would imply the destruction of life by the hands of another; no, in Hell it is the soul itself that tears itself in pieces, with an inward fire surpassing all torments and all pain. It lasted but a moment, but it seemed to her impossible that she should ever forget it, even if she were to live many years, and the terror of that vision was so greatly upon her as she set it down on paper six years later that the natural warmth of her body was chilled even as she wrote.*

* A detailed study could be made of the various forms which diabolical apparitions have taken to holy persons. From such a study would emerge the fact that Satan, whatever his other demerits, was at least a spirit of considerable ingenuity. He could be alarming as when he appeared to St. Elizabeth of Schönau in the shape of a great black bull; ferocious, as when he bit pieces out of the flesh of Blessed Christina of Strommeln, an unfortunate virgin whom he singled out for his attentions, fastening hot stones on to her body, committing unprintable nuisances against her, and sending his demons to attack her in numbers varying between 91 and 40,050;

It would become tedious to enumerate the constant visions to which Teresa was unwillingly subjected, but without at least indicating them it is impossible to form any picture or estimate of what went on in that troubled mind. Some of these visions, for all her denial of the subjectivity of her visions in general, can naturally be traced to the things she knew or had heard about. Thus when she sees herself on a wide plain alone, surrounded by a multitude of people around armed with spears, swords, daggers, and long rapiers; or sees men fighting on a plain, their faces beautiful and as it were on fire, it is not necessary to look further than the stony uplands of Castile or to remember anything beyond the romances of mediaeval combat.

VI

IT is true that these particular experiences, and many others with which she would not trouble her confessor, took place several years after she had entered her second convent, of the Encarnacion, but, even in anticipation, they serve to reveal the stuff of which her fears were made. Ill-health and its consequences came also to hasten her steps towards the cloister. No doubt modern medical knowledge and also modern studies in psychology would supply their own interpretation to explain many of the complicated inter-reactions between Teresa's physical and mental states, and no doubt much of it would be enlightening even if only partially true. There is still something which eludes the scientific explanation, and still something which eludes the historical explanation too, of the age she lived in, the fanatical Spain of the Inquisition when heresy was the Devil's direct work and the laceration of the flesh of no account compared with the danger to the soul.

Illness drove her from Sta Maria de Gracia, first back to her father's house and then to convalesce in the country house of her sister at

mischievous, as when in the form of a mouse he gnawed the thread on the distaff of St. Gertrude of Nivelles to make her lose her temper, or repeatedly blew out the candle of St. Genevieve.

Castellanos de la Cañada, about two days' ride from Avila. Both her sister and her brother-in-law had so great an affection for Teresa that they wished to keep her always with them; but on the road she had broken her journey to stay with an uncle, a most excellent man whose conversation and reading made an important impression upon her uneasy mind. He made her read aloud to him, and although she "did not much like" his books, she characteristically pretended to enjoy them, for it had always been her practice to please others. The good books and the elevated conversation did their work, for God against her own will constrained her to do violence to herself, and three months of struggle (*batalla*) followed as a direct result of this short sojourn in the feudal and arcaded manor-house among the scrub-oak and pines of Hortigosa.

Shortly after her return home, Teresa informed her father of her decision to enter a convent. She was his favourite child, and the announcement was ill received. It therefore became necessary for her to run away again, which she did with greater effect than had resulted from her previous escapade. Once more she enlisted one of her brothers as an accomplice, and, what is more, prevailed upon him to become a friar at the same time. It was not without sorrow that she left her father's house very early in the morning; indeed, she could not believe that the pain of dying would be greater, for it seemed to her as if every bone in her body were wrenched asunder, and, as she had no love for God to destroy her love for her father and kindred, this latter love came upon her with great violence. She thought more, however, of the salvation of her soul, and in this manner her strangely reluctant resolution was finally accomplished.

Finally, yes, but not without breaks and interruptions. During her time of struggle the Devil had already suggested as a deterrent that her health might not stand the strain and privations of the monastic life, a suggestion which proved to be perfectly correct. She had not been for quite two years in the Encarnacion when, although already a professed nun, her fainting-fits and heart-attacks became so frequent and alarming that she was removed first to her sister's country house and then to the village of Becedas, where she was subjected to the excruciating mediaeval treatment of a *curandera* or medicine-woman, renowned in Castile for her cures but worse than powerless to bring any help to Teresa. The patient herself thought the treatment too severe for her constitution. This was putting it mildly, for after two months she felt her life to be nearly worn out; the pain in her heart was such that it seemed to be seized by sharp teeth and it was feared that the torment might end in madness. She could neither sleep nor eat, only drink; she was never without fever, and so reduced owing to the violent purgatives they had given her daily, that her sinews began to shrink and she was in pain from her head down to her feet. Her physicians, when at last her father removed her from the *curandera* and took her back to Avila, declared that the pain from her shrunken nerves must be intolerable; but despite their sympathy they could do nothing for her; came to the conclusion that she must be consumptive, and gave her up as beyond their skill.

A frightful crisis followed. For four whole days she remained in a state of insensibility; the sacrament of Extreme Unction was administered; and "they did nothing but repeat the Credo, as if I could have understood anything they said." The friars at a neighbouring monastery recited the funeral solemnities; a grave was dug at the Encarnacion ready to receive her body and some nuns were actually sent to fetch her away for burial. It is said that her brother, left to keep vigil one night over his supposedly dead sister, fell asleep and overturned a candle, setting fire to the bed clothes, but even this failed to rouse her. They certainly regarded her as dead, for when she finally revived at the end of the four days she had the unusual experience of finding that her eyelids had been sealed with wax. Fortunately her father alone remained obstinate, keeping his finger on her pulse (*que sabia mucho de pulso*) and insisting that his daughter was not yet for the sepulchre.

But when she did come to her senses, in what a terrible condition did she find herself! She had bitten her tongue to pieces; there was such a choking in her throat that she could not swallow even a drop of water; her bones all seemed to be out of joint and the disorder in her head extreme. She was "bent together like a coil of ropes," unable to move either arm or foot or hand or head unless others moved her, and this they had to do suspending her in a sheet, one holding one end and another the other, for she was so bruised (*lastimada*) that she could not endure to be touched. If no one came near her, her pain sometimes ceased and gave her a little rest, though even so it would return during the cold fits of a violent and intermittent fever.

In this condition she had herself carried back to her convent, where "they received alive one whom they had waited for as dead." Her body, she says, was worse than dead, and the sight of it could only give pain, for it was nothing but bones. For three years she remained semi-paralysed, thankful to God when she could begin to crawl about on her hands and knees. It is a shocking contrast with the plump, carefree, vivacious girl in her orange and black velvet frock who had diverted herself so effectively with her cousins in the palace of her youth. Yet, even now, she was only twenty-four.

The question of course arises in the mind: what really ailed her? What malady or maladies produced these fearful effects of emaciation, insensibility, paralysis, cardiac agony, fever, and pains in the head which often drove her to distraction? To what extent were her disorders physical or pathological? Were they due to a combination of genuine physical infirmity aggravated by the nervous tension of her most peculiar temperament? The truth probably lies in this hypothesis. The mental and the physical are in some cases inexplicably mixed up; inexplicably, that is, to the incomplete attainments of our so-far knowledge. Are we perhaps putting the cart before the horse in ascribing the mental disturbance to physical causes, and would it not be truer to say that a mental composition of such excessive sensibility produced so severe a strain that the body inevitably paid? Or was it that a low physical resistance impaired the control and balance of the mind? Impaired is perhaps not the right word, since the spiritual gain of such unspeakable benefit could not be purchased at too high a price.

Furthermore, it must be emphasised that Teresa was not at all the type of *malade imaginaire*. On the contrary she was exasperated by her ill health and by the interruption it brought to whatever matter she might have in hand. She neither desired it nor gloried in it, any more than she desired her raptures or gloried in them except in so far as she welcomed them as a grace from God. In her sensible way she would not despise the remedy of medicine, "I never fail to take that which I see to be necessary for me. May our Lord grant that I do not take more than is necessary —I am afraid I do." Yet in spite of this concession, she disregarded her infirmities as far as possible, and even practised a kind of Christian Science of her own: "My health has been much better since I have ceased to look after my

ease and comforts. It is of great importance not to let our thoughts
frighten us in the beginning. Believe me in this, for I know it by
experience." That is not the language of hysteria, a subject on which
she had many tart and rational things to say when she observed its
occurrence in other people. But it is interesting nevertheless to make
out the formidable list of complaints from which she chronically
suffered. There were those already mentioned: the paralysis, the
fainting-fits, the prolonged insensibility, the constant fever, the
pains in the heart. In addition to this, she sometimes trembled uncon-
trollably from head to foot; she endured daily sickness which she
had to "bring on with a feather" to reduce the pain; quinsy and sore
throats; and, above all, intense headaches and chronic noises in the
head which sometimes made it impossible for her to write and which
she describes as "a number of rushing waterfalls within my brain,
while in other parts, drowned by the noise of the waters, are the
voices of birds singing and whistling." It does not sound too unpleasant, but it occasioned Teresa great distress. She was convinced,
however, that her raptures improved her bodily condition, a conclusion she came to after careful study—"I do not think that it is fancy,
for I have considered the matter and reflected on it."

When she caught influenza, as she did during the epidemic of 1580,
she very nearly died. Doctors had told her that she was consumptive;
it has been suggested also that she was epileptic. It will be remembered
that the detailed description of her personal appearance states that
her eyes were swollen and the front of her throat thickened, which
seems to point to the probability of her being thyrodic. It is stated
by a contemporary writer that she had an open wound in her throat,
which bled whenever she ate. The reason is not given, but is it possible
that some operation had been performed?

She remarks also that she was affected by the moon. "My throat
is better and I have not felt so well for some time, for I can eat almost
without pain, and as the moon is full I consider this a great boon."
And again, "The moon is full: I passed a very bad night and am suffering severely with my head to-day. I have been better until now;
to-morrow, when the moon begins to wane, my health will im-
prove." It is, of course, no old wives' tale, but a fact, that some persons
are thus affected.

Such, then, without touching here on the physical effects observed during her trances, common to all visionaries, was the troublesome constitution of St. Teresa. Obviously the majority of her afflictions arose from what we should call neuropathic causes. But the major mystery still remains unsolved: what is mysticism? what makes the mystic? It is easy to understand the intense desire for union with God; the passionate longing for the submergence of self in the infinite; the wish to enter that state of pure receptivity where such union, such absorption, such loss of self, become possible; that "fierce ardour," as Jan van Ruysbroeck called it, "by which some men are at times caught into the spirit, above the senses." But however consuming the desire, its fulfilment is not to be attained through deliberate effort. "Let the will," said Teresa, "quietly and wisely understand that it is not by dint of labour on our part that we can converse to any good purpose with God, and that our own efforts are only great logs of wood, laid on without discretion to quench this little spark." Something which cannot be commanded must come from without; must come from those unfathomable regions which may contain the august and comprehensive answer to every question. The majority of writers on this subject naturally take as their point of departure the assumption that all such revelations proceed from God (providing, of course, that they do not proceed from the Devil), a demonstrably incorrect hypothesis, since the fixation of the visionary is not necessarily associated with either the divine or its converse, and still less necessarily with the doctrine of Christianity or such usual preoccupations as the passion of Christ or the actuality of the Holy Trinity. Mysticism was known to the Greeks; the word itself has a Greek root; and all that has happened is that a confusion has arisen by which, especially in the minds of theologians, mysticism is now connected almost to a synonymous degree with the revelation of the divine. We are not, however, concerned here with any form of mysticism save that which takes its being from the "religious" impulse in general and the Christian conception of religion in particular. In one sense it is a field of enormous mystery and removedness; but in another sense it holds the simplicity of all great things; the maximum simplicity, even, since its concern is with the greatest of all. Life presents itself under other aspects, important, urgent, immediate, but however momentous, however instant, they are temporal and temporary and of a nature to vanish in a flash under any cosmic catastrophe while the other would still remain. By the other we touch something which is quite different from anything else; we touch nothing less than the absolute, the ultimate reality with no boundary beyond which we can further probe. Even science, in all its forms, is presumably finite; but this other is transcendental and all-embracing in a sense denied to all other expression.

To the detached and objective observer, unaffected by similar convictions, "religion" may often appear strangely dissociated from applied Christianity, if by applied Christianity we mean practical unselfishness, moral charity, and active ministration extended to our neighbour according to our different abilities. In the higher stages of religion, it may even appear that an absorption in personal advancement (in the spiritual sense of course) is the main object which even the theory of expiation for the sins of others can do little in the human sense to justify. St. Ignatius Loyola had definitely laid down in the Constitutions of his Society that nothing so much qualified a minister of God to save others as the sanctification of his own soul in the first place. To the ordinary person, such pursuit may involve a charge of incomprehensible egotism. Life, such persons will argue, is a strenuous and painful business; duty demands that each shall play his part and pull his weight; any form of escape is an evasion, a refusal, glorify it by whatever name you will. Such arguments are as idle as the argument of the Philistine against the aesthetic and we may well believe that the condition of the artist in moments of creative inspiration, the "fine frenzy," is closely comparable to the rapture of the mystic; that the two experiences, in fact, are similar in their nature though perhaps not consciously in their aim. It is no more possible to explain or define beauty, whether aesthetic or natural, to the man without response in his being, than it is possible to blow a flame of inward comprehension of spiritual perception where no spark exists. As little would avail the most careful diagram of a violin, to one who had never heard the sound.

The mystics themselves have dwelt on the hopelessness of the attempt to translate their experiences into intelligible words. Like the poet, they must take refuge in symbol and metaphor, more potent than dry affirmation, more evocative than statement; "I shall have to make use of a comparison," writes St. Teresa; "I should like to

avoid it, but this language of spirituality is so difficult of utterance."
The language of mystical theology is in fact largely and inevitably
metaphorical, since in order to convey any sense of an experience
so entirely outside normal life it is necessary to employ the nearest
possible illustration which comes within the normal range, or, as
a modern writer has indicated, symbolism "attempts to convey a
supernatural experience in the language of visible things . . . used
not for its common purpose but for the associations which it evokes
of a reality beyond the senses." Only by such devices may some
dim reflection of the reality, as in a mirror, be obtained. Hence, the
Church is the bride of Christ; the soul is the bride of Christ; the
soul is a castle with many rooms; the state of rapture is a flight, "a
sweet flight, a delicious flight—a flight without noise;" the mystery
of Godhead is a cloud, "The Cloud of unknowing;" the withdrawal
of God plunges the soul into night, the "Dark night" of St. John of
the Cross. The use of such symbols certainly storms the understanding
more energetically than the definitions compiled by learned bodies
such as the *Societé française de Philosophie* or the Teresian Congress
of Madrid. Yet definitions have been found helpful in establishing
the confused phraseology in current use. Mysticism appears as "Belief
in the possibility of an intimate and direct union between the human
spirit and the fundamental principle of the being, a union which
constitutes at one and the same time a mode of existence and a method
of knowledge foreign and superior to normal existence and normal
knowledge;" or, alternately, as "any interior state which, in the
eyes of the subject, appears as a contact (not through the senses, but
'immediate' and 'intuitive') or as a union of self with something
greater than self, which may be called the soul of the world, God,
or the Absolute according to choice."

The answer, then, to the question what is mysticism? what makes
the mystic? would seem to be either that it is a matter of temperament,
as inexplicable as the temperament of the creative artist; or, as believers will prefer to put it, a direct intervention of God inspiring
the spirit with the revelation of truth. Such intervention, such revelation, may have nothing to do with the conscious desire of the chosen
instrument. Vessels of grace are, apparently, arbitrarily chosen; in
some cases, indeed, surprised and reluctant. Beyond this we cannot
go. But it may be worth noting, since we have already mentioned

the word hysteria in connexion with St. Teresa, that this word is popularly employed in a loose and misleading sense, to suggest the ranting excitability of uncontrolled emotion. In a truer sense it should be employed to denote a most variable form of neurosis, capable of producing either a complete disintegration of personality, or a schizophrenic condition of personality, or a psychological disposition inclining the subject towards involuntary auto-suggestion which may take a base and deplorable form or a form most spiritual and lofty. In parenthesis, and still with a reverent acknowledgment of the theory that mystical experience originates with the intervention of God, it is tempting to speculate on the inherent probability of this belief as opposed to the equally possible subjectivity of supernatural manifestations. In other words, is it or is it not conceivable that in the hypothetical case of a person who had never heard of God, Christ, the Communion of Saints, the Devil, or any of the accepted appurtenances of religion, the phenomenon of divine visions or locutions should occur? It is a pregnant though perhaps subversive question. Is it possible to imagine a stigmatist to whom the story of the Crucifixion should be totally unknown? Is it possible to imagine our Lady appearing to one who was unacquainted with the story of Christ's nativity? If such cases exist, proven beyond suspicion, they would seem to settle the matter once and for all; but in their absence it would seem logical to conclude that the phenomena of mystical theology must take their origin from some image already in the mind.

This conclusion, of course, does not affect either the sincerity of the subject or the verity of some great mystery, veiled from most eyes, but accessible in moments of revelation to the few. It affects only the form in which such revelations are enwrapped.*

* St. Bernadette Soubirous maintained that our Lady said to her, "I am the Immaculate Conception," and that she had never heard the expression and did not know what it meant. This would appear to be a close approach to our hypothetical case, but, without casting any doubt on St. Bernadette's integrity, it is impossible to be certain that she had not heard or read the words somewhere, although she may not consciously have registered them in her mind.

VII

TERESA at any rate was innocent of fraudulence or of conscious self-suggestion. She was more than innocent, she was sceptical and alarmed, and her doubts were increased by the incapacity of her earlier confessors and advisers who sometimes cautioned her and sometimes encouraged her, so that she did not know what to believe, and was in great fear, and could not refrain from tears. What distressed her most of all was the command always to make the sign of the cross when she had a vision of heavenly nature—for these occurred even more frequently than the frankly satanic visions—to be persuaded of its diabolic origin, and to point her finger at it in scorn. "To point the finger," a recognised method for averting evil, is done by doubling the fist and allowing the tip of the thumb to protrude between the index and the middle finger, or the gesture may be made by means of a charm, such as fill the coral and tortoiseshell shops at Naples. One such object, traditionally said to have been used by Teresa, is preserved at the convent of Medina del Campo, a little horn of flint, an inch and a half long, mounted in silver. Teresa, under her vow of obedience and in her Catholic acceptance of the dictum that priests and confessors spoke with the authority of God and knew better than she, did as she was bidden, though it was a fearful thing for her to do, as she could not believe that the vision did not come from God, and it was most painful for her to make a show of contempt whenever she saw our Lord: it reminded her of the insults the Jews had heaped upon Him. In fact, she could not always bring herself continually to the gesture, so evaded the command at times by the expedient of holding a crucifix in her hand. This crucifix, and the rosary to which it was attached, our Lord took once from her, and returned it, no longer made of ebony, but of four large stones more beautiful than diamonds. "They were seen, however, by no one else—only by myself."

After she had been commanded to put her visions to such tests and to resist them with all her power, they only increased in convincingness and frequency. It was in vain that she tried to distract herself and made piteous complaints to our Lord, telling Him that she could bear no more; her prayers were disregarded and she continued to experience the ineffable sweetness and excessive pain, so great that it made her moan, so sweet that she could not wish to be rid of it. Somewhere in her soul, though it was an insubordination greatly to be deprecated, persisted the conviction that she was better advised than her confessors. She took the problem to our Lord, who reassured her, for although He would not release her from her obedience, He helped her in another way by teaching her what she was to say, and gave her reasons so sufficient that she began to feel herself to be perfectly safe. Moreover, He sent her a practical comfort in the shape of St. Peter of Alcantara, who, although he lived in a cell only four and a half feet in length, trained himself not to sleep more than an hour and a half out of the twenty-four, ate but once in three days (a mere nothing, compared with St. Simeon Stylites who passed the whole forty days of Lent without touching food), never raised his eyes from the ground or looked on a woman's face, and wore continually a girdle of pointed wire, still "with all his sanctity, he was very agreeable." He listened gravely to Teresa's account of her troubles, which she gave him, she says, as briefly as she could, though, knowing her volubility both in speech and on paper, we may doubt if it was very brief; comforted her greatly, threw light on many dark matters, and paid her the supreme compliment of returning her confidence. They parted fast friends, with the understanding that she should write to him and that they should pray for one another. He predeceased her by twenty years, but the change-over into another world was negligible, for he frequently appeared to her and she found that she received even more help and consolation from him after his entrance into the heavenly city than when he was on earth.

This terror lest supernatural visions should be a delusion of the Devil is common to all sincere persons thus affected, and to their spiritual directors, but none ever suffered more keenly than Teresa of Avila. A long section of her autobiography, and many passages in her other works, are devoted to an anguished effort to disentangle truth from possible falsehood and also—once the fact of divine revelation has been accepted—to distinguish between the various mental and spiritual states in which manifestations occur. It is at this point that the lay reader begins to marvel at the infinite elaboration of mystical writing. The fundamental idea seems so simple in plain statement, difficult though it may be of attainment; but even as the amateur inevitably grows impatient with what he regards as the superfluous discriminations of the expert, exclaiming that the connoisseur has lost his "sense of beauty" through an excessive interest in the variations and niceties of technique, so does the ordinary reader clasp his head in bewilderment, introduced to a region of theological metaphysics which appears only to confuse and not to clarify, as it should, the original issue. Led through successive stages of contemplation and of prayer; thinking that he is at last nearing the peak, only to find himself back somewhere among the foothills, he may be forgiven for beginning to wonder whether there will always be something beyond; whether, when he thinks he is beginning to understand, to grasp the hindermost meaning, he will always be pulled back and humbled into a fresh set of complexities. Alas, if he wishes to persevere with his researches, the sooner he resigns himself to this idea the better. There is apparently no easy road, no short cut; and, like wading out into the sea, the further he wades the deeper will become the water. His only hope is that he may at last learn to swim.

Teresa, true and great mystic though she was, is not quite so baffling as some. Her symbolism is neither so subtle and involved as that of St. John of the Cross, nor her teaching so profound as that of St. Thomas Aquinas. She was not a learned woman. She confessed to knowing nothing of mystical theology and to being ill-grounded in the art of orison. Unlike her male contemporaries she had, of course, attended no school or university; it was sufficiently remarkable that for a woman of her period and race, she should easily read and write at all. She knew Latin so little that she always had to get it translated for her;* her reading was not very extensive, though she is known to have read *The Imitation of Christ*, the letters of St. Jerome, the *Moralia* of St. Gregory, and probably *The Confessions* of St. Augustine; reading indeed, although she had always been fond of it, was difficult for her, for she found that whenever she took up a book she became "recollected" through it and her pleasure was turned to prayer. By nature an intellectual, as Crashaw so rightly indicated, she had for various reasons been denied the advantages which every intellectual should enjoy. Those large draughts of illumination to which he referred were

---

* She makes a curious statement, to the effect that, when in the prayer of quiet, she "who scarcely understand a word of what I read in Latin, understand the Latin as if it were Spanish."

the outcome not so much of education, as of her own analytical mind. Here was a woman surprised by her own experiences, endeavouring to set them down for her own enlightenment, for the information of her confessors, or for the guidance of her nuns. Working out her own explanation in this way, she frequently grew confused and repetitive, and was apologetically conscious of the fault, but a glance at the difficult conditions under which she composed her works must greatly soften the impatience of the reader. Teresa, in fact, was trying to live two different lives at the same time: the life of action and the life of contemplation. Only a very muscular personality such as hers could force the two into any compatibility at all. Her writing was perpetually interrupted by the demands of her duties; her duties were perpetually disturbed by the onslaught of her mystical experience. "Such a book requires leisure," she wrote of the *Way of Perfection*; "as you know, I have so little that I have been unable to go on with it for a week, and I forget both what I have written and how I intended to continue."

The actual physical inconvenience she suffered when writing was perhaps the thing that troubled her least of all. Yet many people would find it a considerable interference with the flow of thought. *The Way of Perfection* was composed in a cell with no table and no chair; she had either to kneel or sit on the floor. Her paper lay on a ledge under the window; but that window had no glass, it had only canvas stretched on a frame to keep out the bitter winds of Avila, and thus, to all intents and purposes, was permanently open, numbing a scribbler who was painfully sensitive to cold. The composition of *The Interior Castle* was hampered in a manner perhaps even more troublesome. This exquisitely iridescent book provides a supreme instance of inspirational writing, though, unfortunately for the author, she was not privileged to indulge in an orgy of concentration such as Handel could allow himself during the bringing forth of his *Messiah*. Inspirational indeed it was, and that we know, partly from the account of those who saw her at work, partly from the extraordinary rapidity with which she wrote it. It was said that, on returning from an ecstasy, she sometimes found written pages which she thought were not her own; yet the manuscript shows no difference in the handwriting. "I know not what I am saying," she wrote once, "for I am writing this as if the words were not mine." Those who saw her at work, nuns of the

Segovia convent, whether posted at her door or coming to interrupt her with messages, deposed that she wrote without stopping to erase or correct, her face irradiated by a light that faded when she laid her pen aside, so that in comparison it seemed like darkness; or so absorbed that she failed to observe the entry of a messenger into her cell. "Sit down, my child," she said when at last her attention had been attracted, "and let me write what our Lord has told me before I forget it." It must have been alarming to be sent on an errand to the Foundress on such occasions. Not that she ever gave way to irritability, enduring always with patience. But Mother Mary of the Nativity, at the convent of Toledo, coming in with a message just as Teresa was starting on a new sheet, was terrified to see that the saint, after removing her spectacles to listen to the message, was then seized in a trance lasting several hours. The nun dared not move or go away, but remained staring at Teresa until she finally came to her senses. The blank sheet of paper by this time was covered with writing, and Teresa, noticing this herself and aware that the nun also had noticed it, put the paper away without comment into a box. It had never been her practice to advertise her peculiar seizures, but rather to pass them over as though they had not occurred.

As for the rapidity of her composition, she wrote the *Interior Castle*, a work of two hundred and sixty printed pages, or about the length of the average novel, in four weeks. This is itself would be an unusual feat, even for a work of fiction where the pen has only to run as fast as it can in pursuit of the invention and no hard processes of thought are necessary, but a theological treatise involving a symbolical exposition of the progressive states of the soul in prayer is a different matter. Add to this, that the period was included in one of the most uphill times Teresa ever passed through; she was ill, everything was going against her Reform, she was worried by opposition and busy with urgent affairs; and, as though that were not enough, her election as Prioress to the Encarnacion, with its attendant tumult, coincided also. The writing of the book, in consequence, was interrupted for five months; that is to say, she gave a fortnight to the execution of the first half and a fortnight to the execution of the second—a disturbing break which will arouse the sympathy of any author. Her power of concentration must have been amazing. She must have had the gift of devoting herself absorbedly to whatever she was doing, whether it was the foundation of a new convent or the examination of the most abstruse spiritual problems, to the momentary exclusion of everything else—a respect in which she evidently did not resemble a fellow-theologian and saint, Thomas Aquinas, who could become so lost in irrelevant thoughts that when dining with the King of France he heard nothing of the conversation going on around him, but suddenly thumped the table with his fist, exclaiming, "Ha! that settles the Manichees!"

Teresa was not like that. Yet she was familiar with the jangle of the nerves resultant on the broken spell, the precious mood destroyed, so delicate to create, so laborious to recapture. Coleridge, for ever losing the completion of *Kubla Khan* through the intrusion of the person who came on business from Porlock, was under the influence of a drug, it is true; but Teresa was under the influence of a supernatural drug more potent than any delusions or imaginations of laudanum.

Most curious, incidentally, is her remark upon resuming the work that her head was too weak to read over what she had already written and that no doubt it will be very disconnected and full of repetitions as a result; adding, not very politely, that as it is only for her sisters, it will matter little. It must be rare that authorship should be undertaken in so casual, even negligent, a spirit; but the subject was in fact so intrinsic a part of Teresa's mind, that she had only to place her paper over her mind as it were, and make a tracing of the inspired script she found already engraved there. God Himself had supplied the basic image around which she built her Castle. He had shown her, in one of the loveliest and most lyrical visions she ever had, exactly how she should construct this habitation of the soul, from the precincts crawling with the reptiles of evil to the central hall where the Source of Light sat gloriously enthroned. The precincts were horrible indeed, and must have struck very forcibly into the imagination of Spanish nuns familiar with such poisonous creatures as salamanders, tarantulas, and other creeping darting dangers of daily life; "a mass of darkness and impurity, full of toads and vipers and other venomous animals"; but, once the infested entrance had been passed, God showed her "a most beautiful globe of crystal in the shape of a castle, with seven rooms, the seventh, situated in the centre, being occupied by the King of Glory, resplendent with the most exquisite brilliancy which

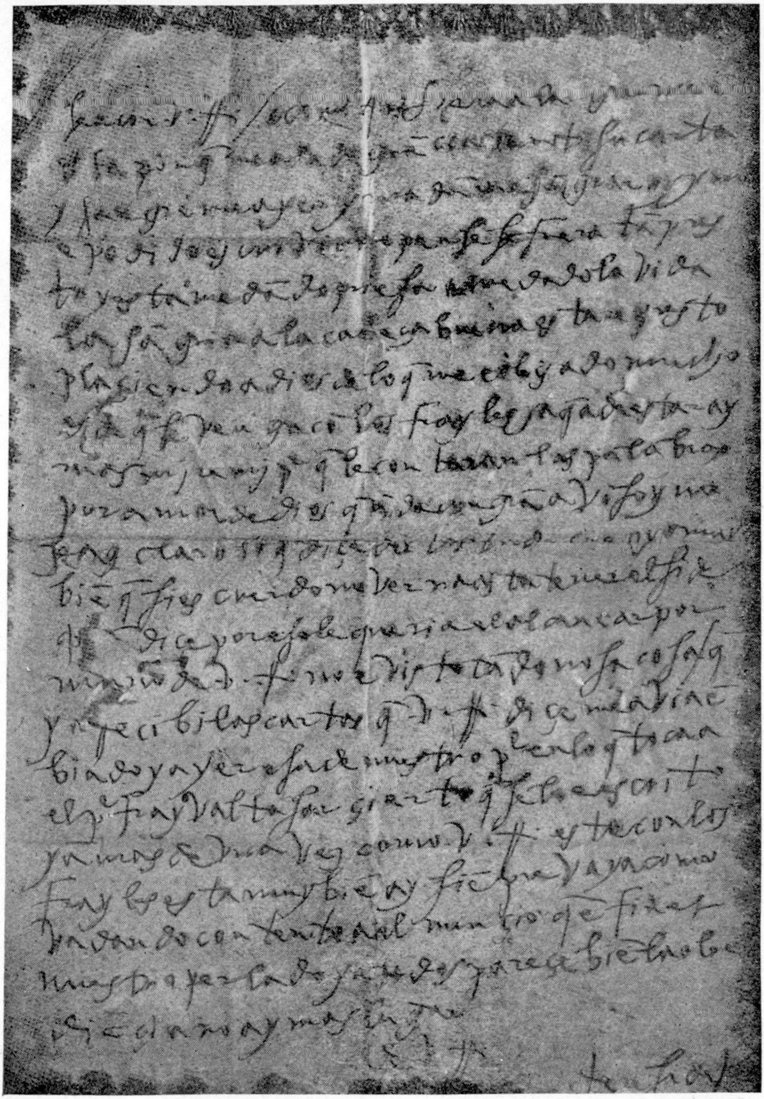

A LETTER FROM ST. TERESA

El Greco.

TOLEDO IN A STORM

shone through and adorned the adjoining rooms. The nearer these lay to the centre, the more did they partake of that wondrous light." She was still admiring this beauty which by the grace of God dwells in the soul, when the light suddenly disappeared and the crystal became opaque and dark as coal, emitting an intolerable stench, and the venomous animals, formerly held in check outside, obtained admittance into the castle. Teresa thought that everyone should share in this vision, for in her opinion no one having once beheld such splendour and grace, forfeited by sin and replaced by such repulsive misery, would ever again dare to offend God.

She related this vision to her confessor the very day that it occurred to her, but characteristically regretted her impulsive indiscretion as soon as she had slept on it. "How I forgot myself yesterday!" she said to him next morning. "I cannot think how it could have happened. Those high aspirations of mine and the affection I have for you must have caused me to go beyond all reasonable limits." He promised her faithfully to say nothing about it during her lifetime, though after her death he felt impelled to make it known to all men.

VIII

IT will become apparent from all this that another side to the picture existed, very different from those bloodshot and appalling visions of Satan and his Hell. There was the ineffably radiant vision of Christ and His Heaven. Christ stood before her, "stern and grave," admonishing her; sometimes He showed her nothing but His hands, the beauty of which was so great that no language could describe it; when He showed her the wound in that beautiful hand, and drew out the great nail that was in it, so that it seemed to her He also tore the flesh, she was naturally much distressed, but understood that any suffering she might be called upon to endure was a trifle compared with the pain that He had borne. Sometimes it was the whole Sacred Humanity that she saw, but this she could not bear to describe without doing great violence to herself, and confined herself to saying that He seemed then as the painters represent Him after the Resurrection in beauty and

D

majesty. Often He spoke to her, now with reproach and now with encouragement, filling her with "exceeding strength and earnestness of purpose," so that she thought she could rise above every possible hindrance put in her way, and leaving her also with the understanding of what it was for a soul to be walking in the truth, in the presence of Truth itself.

These visions and locutions were to Teresa a source of mingled worry and joy. At long last she came to accept them as the true appearance of the divine presence, but even then her analytical mind continued to ferret after the explanation of their exact nature. Painstakingly, in page after page, paragraph after paragraph, she tries to define. Is it a bodily or an intellectual vision? She thinks she does not see with her bodily eyes, not even with the eyes of the soul. Even this is too crude a differentiation to satisfy her, and she must split it again: it seems that there are three kinds of visions, the bodily, the imaginary, and the intellectual, of which the bodily is the lowest, the intellectual the highest, and the imaginary half-way between the two. In this, despite her avowed ignorance of theological science, she had arrived perhaps unwittingly at the same conclusion as the scholastics, who placed the imagination between the senses and the intellect, receiving impressions from the former and transmitting them to the latter. Corporal visions and locutions are dangerous enough, but less so than imaginary visions and locutions, for these are so closely associated with the memory that the seer can never be sure that they do not derive merely from things once seen or heard; and deception, perhaps unintentional, may easily arise. St Thomas Aquinas had distinguished very severely: the vision of Isaiah, and the apocalyptic revelation of St. John, were all imaginary; and as for the appearances of Christ to the women and the apostles after the resurrection, those were apparitions and not visions at all. It was important, nevertheless, to make yet another distinction between visions, apparitions and hallucinations, for hallucinations were the product of a morbid state in which a physical condition threw the memory into disorder, causing it to reproduce in a valueless way things which it already contained. The intellectual vision was the purest and loftiest of all, for no part was played by either the imagination or the memory, and certainly not by the senses, the bodily eyes not seeing, the bodily ears not hearing, but the whole spirit infused by what Teresa called the feeling of the presence of

God, when the soul was suspended in such a way that it seemed to be utterly beside itself; the memory lost; the understanding not lost, but not at work, making no reflections, merely standing as if amazed at the greatness of the things it understands. This is almost the same as saying that intuition is superior to reason, the spiritual opposed to the human; thoughts, as Teresa put it, obviously setting thoughts on the lower plane, not being the same thing as the understanding. Not the same thing, and not so fine, so rarefied a thing.

Teresa was very certain that her experiences were neither bodily nor hallucinatory; she does not seem to have been so sure that they were not imaginary as opposed to intellectual. (By "imaginary" she, of course, did not mean delusive, or invented, but was using the word in its theologically technical sense.) But her humility was always extreme, and to others it may appear that they were of the highest order; the point is scarcely worth arguing about. It is of greater interest to examine what Teresa has to say of this extraordinary interior life which doubled her active and practical existence. She was utterly convinced of the reality of her experiences for two reasons, which she constantly emphasises in the most vigorous language at her command—and the driving force of her language could be very vigorous indeed. The first reason is that her visions were not sought by her; she did not seek to provoke them, and in fact knew from experience that any such attempt was idle. She had tried it in the days when fear ruled her and she longed only for the healing love of God to sustain her, but although she laboured with all her might to imagine Jesus Christ present within her, and to picture His Humanity, she never could do it. Later, when she had ceased to try, the intensity of the Presence repeatedly overwhelmed her, often causing her acute embarrassment. Far from endeavouring deliberately to think herself into a state of spirituality, she now sought only to safeguard herself, but "these little precautions are of no use when our Lord will have it otherwise." No amount of quotation can convey any suggestion of how constant was this worry in her mind, or of how pitifully she tried to appear as a normal person in her outward life. It is as though she regarded her transports as a solecism, an offence against polite and well-bred manners. "These ecstasies come upon me with great violence and in such a way as to be outwardly visible, I having no power to resist them, even when I am with others, for they come in such a way as admits of no disguising them unless it be by letting people suppose that, as I am subject to disease of the heart, they are fainting fits. I take great pains to resist them when they are coming on—sometimes I cannot do it." And again, "I was so unwell that I thought I might be excused making my prayer, but . . . I was rapt in spirit with such violence that I could make no resistance whatsoever." She wrote to her brother that she felt so utterly ashamed, she wanted to hide herself, no matter where; and, being a practical woman, added that if this spiritual state, which has already lasted a week, continues, it will cause her ill success with her many business affairs. She has prayed earnestly that she may no longer have raptures in public, and asks her brother to pray about it too, "for these are many disadvantages." Occasionally she has been able, by great efforts, to make a slight resistance; but afterwards she has felt worn out like a person who has been contending with a strong giant.

The physical effects of these transports were often exceedingly troublesome, especially to a person who in no way wanted to make an exhibition of herself. There were occasions when, unaware of what was taking place, frightened people tried to use force on the rigid body. The sister-sacristan at Toledo found her leaning against a wall after receiving Holy Communion, stiff and hard as stone, and exerted all her strength to make her sit down, dragging at her by both hands, but until Teresa came to herself there was no budging her. The nuns at Avila had likewise had difficulty in removing her from the grille after communicating. Sisters in various convents recorded their alarm at the state in which they found her. Sometimes her pulse had ceased to beat at all, her bones were racked, and her hands so rigid that she could not join them. Sometimes she used such force to prevent herself from entering into this condition that she felt afterwards as though all her bones had been broken, and at other times she would shut herself into her cell at the signal for prayer, making no reply if anyone knocked at the door. In whatever position she was when the rapture overcame her, in that position did she continue until she regained command of her senses, sitting, standing, or kneeling; the body lost its natural warmth; and the hands became as hard as pieces of wood. One of her nuns, finding her alone in this condition in the garden of the convent, remonstrated with her for endangering her life by undergoing such trials, only to be met with the tart rejoinder, "Hold your

peace, child; do you think that this depends upon myself?" Indeed it
did not. Nor did that strange phenomenon known as levitation, to
which she was most liable and which seems to have alarmed her more
than anything else. Her body would then become buoyant, as if all
weight had departed from it; a great force beneath her feet lifted her
up, and she could clearly be seen to leave the ground. She would do
everything in her power to prevent this from happening, for she
thought it "a most extraordinary thing, which would occasion much
talk," and commanded her nuns never to speak of it, but conceal it
from them she could not. Sometimes she threw herself on the ground
to avert the happening and they would cluster round her to hold her
down; at other times she would clutch with both hands at an iron
grating. It was bad enough when it occurred in the presence of her
own community, but when strangers were witnesses she was not to
be comforted; and would speak of her weak heart, or ask for a little
water or some food in the attempt to make everything appear natural.
Levitation is no uncommon prodigy,[*] and is ascribed on good evidence
to over two hundred saints and other persons, so that the Bishop of
Avila was probably not much surprised when he saw Teresa lifted
into the air during Mass, but to Teresa herself it was one of the greatest
shames and inconveniences she had to suffer. It seems curious, considering how subject she was to these various physical phenomena,
that she should never have completed them by receiving the stigmata.

IX

TROUBLED beholder though she was, Teresa naturally derived an unspeakable inner joy from this constant communion with a region
which to her was of such crowning importance. It is unnecessary and
perhaps also impossible to suggest what the privilege of such access
must mean to the believer. To know oneself for one of the elect

[*] See, for instance, Ezekiel, chap. 8, verse 3. Among "popular" saints, the
example of St. Catherine of Siena is well known, but for something a little
more out of the way, see Appendix 1, p. 176, for an account of the truly extraordinary case of St. Joseph of Cupertino.

despite the humbling sense of unworthiness that goes with such knowledge; despite the humility that in face of such a light abases one, dazzled, to the ground; to know that for oneself, inexplicably, in one's lowliness, a corner of the curtain is drawn aside; to perceive for one-self the presentation of such recondite mysteries; to touch the ultimate secret; to account, through a revealed faith, for the unaccountable; to hear intelligibly the voice of the unintelligible God; to see the bodily semblance of the hidden God; to be privy to that which is concealed from all men, and which may yet comprise the answer to all science, all philosophy, all art, all searching—this, no less, is the possession of the mystic. "Oh my God," said Teresa, "how different from merely hearing these words is it to realise their truth in this way! How different are spiritual matters from anything that can be seen or heard in this world!"

Rapture, she said—and how readily one can believe her—left behind it a strange detachment which she would never be able to describe; a singular estrangement from the things of earth, which made life much more distressing, God so stripping the soul of everything that there was nothing left on earth which could be its companion. The fact of rapture was undeniable, but its details were baffling and de-manded constant examination. Thus although when contemplating the beauty of Christ she much desired to examine the colour of His eyes or to determine His exact stature, she never could do so, for, as she endeavoured to gaze, she lost the vision altogether. Whenever she tried to concentrate on a particular part of the vision, the whole vision vanished. This confession of failure, this radical honesty, this conscientiousness in never pretending to see or hear more than she actually believed she saw and heard, is extremely convincing, and rules out any suggestion that she could delude herself into imagining something which was not "there." Far otherwise. "There are no means of bringing it (the vision) about; there is no possibility of taking anything away from it or of adding to it; nor is there any way of effecting it whatever we may do, nor of seeing it when we like, nor of abstaining from seeing it." She "never knew before that such a thing was possible," and is at pains to understand exactly whence her conviction of the Presence comes. "If I say that I see Him neither with the eyes of the body nor with those of the soul, how is it that I can understand and maintain that He stands beside me and be more certain of it than if I saw Him? I am* like a person who feels that another is close beside her, but because I am in the dark I see him not, yet am certain that he is there present. Still, this comparison is not exact; for he who is in the dark, in some way or other, through hearing a noise or having seen that person before, knows he is there; but here there is nothing of the kind, for without a word inward or outward, the soul clearly perceives who it is, where He is, and occasionally what He means. He renders Himself present to the soul by a certain knowledge of Himself which is more clear than the sun. I do not mean that we now see either a sun or any brightness, only that there is a light not seen, which illumines the understanding.—All that is written in this paper is the simple truth."

The same applied to locutions, or hearing of the words spoken to her by Christ, whether harsh, comforting, or advisory. "A person commending a matter to God with great earnestness may think that he hears in some way or other whether his prayer will be granted or not, and this is quite possible; but he who has heard the divine locution will see clearly enough the great difference between the two. If it be anything which the understanding has fashioned, however cunningly it may have done so, he sees that it is the understanding which has arranged that locution and that it is speaking of itself. It has not been listening only, but also forming the words. In the locution of God there is no escape. I know this much by experience, for my resistance lasted nearly two years because of the great fear I was in, and even now I resist occasionally; but it is no use."

She was not even sure whether she *heard* the words or not. "I learnt at times by means of words uttered; at other times I learnt some things without the help of words, and that more clearly than those other things which were told me in words. I understood exceedingly deep truths concerning the Truth. . . . The truth of which I am speaking, and which I was given to see, is truth itself, in itself. It has neither beginning nor end. I understand it all, notwithstanding that my words are obscure in comparison with that distinctness."

Her words are obscure perhaps, but only because she was forced into trying to express the inexpressible. Her actual phrasing is always

---

* St. Teresa actually wrote "*She* is like a person," etc., for it was often her habit when making these intimate revelations to refer to herself in the third person.

clear and energetic, even homely, as when she compares her revelations to food received into the stomach which had not first been eaten, without our knowing how it had entered though we know well enough that it is there. St. Teresa provided the oddest mixture between the most abstruse mystical life and rough common sense in trying to deal with it. It was typical of her to cling to iron railings to prevent herself from being supernaturally lifted into the air. Temperamentally, she preferred the ground. Her analogies, even when dealing with matters of high spirituality, are usually drawn from the most realistic sources: if fish are taken from the river in a net they cannot live, and so it is with souls drawn out of the heavenly water; slowness in spiritual progress resembles the pace of a hen; men are like branches of dried rosemary, so brittle that they break when leaned on; she herself is like a parrot which has learned to talk; the soul is like a little ass, which feeds and thrives because it accepts the food given it; those souls who overload themselves with mortifications are like a child loaded with two bushels of corn, who not only cannot carry them but breaks down under the burden and falls. (The precision here is characteristic: Teresa who had spent a good deal of her time on country estates knew that although a child might carry one bushel, it could not carry two.) At times her comparisons have almost the ring of a proverb: those who watch the bull-fight from behind the barrier do not run the same risk as those who expose themselves to the horns; and poverty is strikingly suggested by the phrase "not even a withered leaf to dress a pilchard with." Chess comes in usefully for illustrative purposes, and here again she knew what she was talking about, for a board and men figured in the inventory of her father's possessions; she was rather dubious about taking a game as a simile in religious matters for her nuns, but passed it off with a laugh, "This will show you what a Mother God has given you, skilled even in such vanities as this!" But in addition to this factual, often of-the-soil vividness of expression, she possessed also something of the poet's vision, when her imagery flamed more splendid; and then, God became like to a burning furnace, or to a most brilliant diamond much larger than the whole world, in which all our actions were reflected, or the soul suddenly became bright as a mirror, clear behind, sideways, upwards, and downwards, a sculptured mirror, with Christ in the centre, and the lustre dimmed only as by a vapour when the soul was in mortal sin.

Light and water, and all the qualities attendant on them, possessed a great fascination for Teresa. Child of a dry land, she was peculiarly sensitive to water; a stream, a fountain, or even a well from which water might be drawn by a windlass to refresh the thirsty garden, held for her a lovely and allegorical significance; the element, she said, which she loved so much that she had studied it more attentively than other things. The poet in her responded to the play of light on ripples; the practical Castilian in her responded to the usefulness of irrigation. She could write of "most pellucid water running in a bed of crystal, reflecting the rays of the sun," and she could write also of the four ways in which a garden may be watered, by water taken out of a well which is very laborious, or by water raised in buckets by means of a windlass—she has drawn it thus herself, and finds it less troublesome, also it gives a more copious supply—or by a stream or brook, which is better still for the soil is more thoroughly saturated, there is no necessity to water so often, and the labour of the gardener is less, or by showers of rain which is best of all. However she treats it, the result upon her writings is to produce a strange luminosity which glints over the homespun of her realism and her rough Castilian style. Both *The Interior Castle* and *The Way of Perfection*, apart from their other qualities of profundity, enlightenment, and sagacity both human and spiritual, possess a kind of shimmering beauty made up of water and of light. They are as nacreous as oyster shells, with a prismatic transparency surely reflected from the incandescent certainty at the centre of her soul.*

★ A miraculous and indescribable light is, of course, a very usual accompaniment of sacred revelations. The instances are too numerous to recount here. The image of the mirror is also not uncommon, e.g. St. Joseph of Cupertino who, when asked what souls in ecstasy saw during their raptures, replied, "They feel as though they were taken into a wonderful gallery, shining with never-ending beauty, where in a glass, with a single look, they apprehend the marvellous vision which God is pleased to show them."

Mention must be made of that most remarkable woman, the twelfth-century "Sibyl of the Rhine," St. Hildegard, whose Blake-like visions and drawings, connected with falling angels and splendid stars, are often of great beauty. Mystic, poet, artist, physician, naturalist, psychologist, hers is a biography which should be written.

X

ALTHOUGH Teresa had struggled so painfully, one-half of her energy taken up with resistance and the other half with arguments and self-persuasions against her own inclinations, convent life before she came to interfere with it was not necessarily a thing to be dreaded. Spain at that time was a most curious mixture of laxness on the one hand and of intense bigotry and fanaticism on the other. On the side of fanaticism, the Lutheran heresy had aroused both the apprehension and the conscience of the Catholic Church. Teresa's Spain was the Spain of the Inquisition; one of its first and most ghastly persecution cases had originated in her own city of Avila, and Torquemada himself had found burial there in San Tomás seventeen years before her birth (1498). The Inquisition with its appalling record of cruelty has probably done more than anything else to damage the reputation of the Roman Church in the eyes of non-Catholic communities, more even than the sometimes abused and misused influence exerted by her ministers over ignorant and gullible people. In order to understand the Inquisition at all, though God knows that is difficult enough, it is necessary always to remember two things; first that the Spaniards, according to English standards, are a merciless and violent race to whom physical suffering means very little though physical courage a great deal; and in the second place that the devotion to the salvation of the soul entirely outweighed all considerations of the torment of the body. This is putting it crudely and stating only a twentieth part of what might be said either in condemnation or mitigation. Nor is this the place to dwell in any detail upon the abhorrent persecutions instituted in the name of the Christian faith—the system of informers and secret denunciations, conducted in such an atmosphere of terror that no man could feel safe from his nearest friend, a system morally disastrous even if productive of immediate results in the hunting down of heresy; the scandalous system of bribery by which the Vatican itself could be induced to remit the sentence already passed by the Inquisitors; or to do more than suggest the analogy between the "racial purity" slogan of Nazi Germany and the laws of pure blood (*limpia sangre*) framed in such remarkable anticipation by the courts of the Inquisition. Jews, as well as heretics, were subject to the same outrages; by the edict of Ferdinand and Isabella in 1492 not a Jew was to be left alive in Spain; two hundred thousand of them, perhaps more, stripped of their homes and property, were given four months in which to make good their escape to some other country, but the road to escape was not so easy; to plunder the fugitives was a lucrative virtue, and on the crowded roads leading to the coast or the frontier many a Jew was intercepted and knifed open to discover whether before his departure he had swallowed the remnant of his gold pieces or precious stones.

The similarity with Hitler's Germany is striking, with the only difference that Spain based her persecutions on fanatically religious instead of fanatically nationalist and political grounds. Wherever men feel passionately, the explosion of aggression must ensue; and since there is no subject on which men have felt more passionately than the way in which they shall worship their God and shall compel the compliance of the unwilling, the jealous and enormous power of the Church, directed in this case by a naturally fierce nation, and with the incentive of cupidity added in, was set in motion with all the terrible apparatus of torture both physical and mental against the possible threat to her supreme authority.

At the centre of the web lurked the King in the fastness of the Escorial. The character of Philip II epitomises the more sombre aspects of his own intransigent people. God and Spain shone as the jewels in the dark mind of Philip, who, bracketed with the Pope, knew himself to be the most puissant man in Europe. Seated at his desk, working on the orderly piles of papers, minuting them with his own hand, he brought his tidy, relentless, though hesitating mind to bear both upon policy and detail. Amongst those papers he would sometimes come across a letter signed "Teresa de Jesus, Carmelita." Although these letters were always respectful in tone, usually praying for some favour, the sterner note was not always absent. "Remember, Sire, that Saul was anointed and yet he was rejected. . . ."

The prevailing spirit of religious enthusiasm spread outwards in widening circles, taking less corrupt though equally excessive forms among strange characters up and down the country. While the silken prelates grew fat on their disgraceful booty, obscure men and women in a state of exaltation adopted the most mortifying modes of life to satisfy their craving for self-immolation and, sometimes, for publicity. Tattered figures lay in an ecstasy of prayer in the side-chapels of the churches, sometimes misleading the charitable into a rush to give help; hermits abounded; the daughter of a peasant near Avila lived in such close touch with our Lady that she would always pause on the threshold of a door, with gesture of politeness inviting her to go first. Royalty, the Court, and the nobility were likewise affected; Catalina of the Dukes of Cardona, the governess of Don Carlos and Don John of Austria, disappeared from Court and was found living in a wild beast's den, dressed in sackcloth, sustaining herself on grass and roots; scourging herself frequently for two hours on end with a heavy chain, so that her sackcloth was full of blood; proceeding a quarter of a league to Mass on her knees; and calling herself only *la Pecadora*, the prostitute. Don John himself, though less tempted to extremes, toyed with the idea of entering a monastery; the Princess of Brazil, regent of Spain during the King's absence, shut herself up in her palace and would give audience only veiled from head to foot in black; the young captain Ignatius Loyola hung up his arms in the shrine of our Lady of Monserrat and kept vigil all night before her altar; a young knight of Navarre, Francisco de Xavier, joined forces with him and carried the message of the Church into furthest Asia. The churches were crowded, even in bitter weather, when the devout came carrying the *bolilla*, a little metal ball filled with hot water, to warm their hands. Sorcery was rampant; potions and charms were forthcoming for every requirement; Teresa herself in the endeavour to rescue a priest from the spell his mistress had cast over him, was obliged to lure from him the little copper image he wore and throw it into a river, and, although "as to this matter of enchantment, I do not believe it to be wholly true," yet she was not above hanging the gallstone of an animal round the neck of her confessor to keep him from the harm of his enemies. In this world of superstition and religious excitation, the inhabitants of the overcrowded convents were not always above reproach, whether from a genuine self-delusion (inspired, of course, by the Arch-tempter) or from deliberate imposture. The temptation to impose not only on the credulous but also on priests, confessors, and on the other members of the community, was great and very gratifying in its results, until, as sometimes happened, the Inquisition looked into the matter and sent the culprit to the scaffold or the dungeon. Thus, the oracular Magdalena de la Cruz, a Poor Clare of Cordoba, deceived even the Inquisitor-General to the extent that he begged her prayers on his behalf, and at the humble request of the Empress Isabel she worked with her own hands the christening-robes of the unborn child who was to become Philip II. It was a shock for all when she suddenly announced that from the age of five she had been subject to delusions and that all her prophecies and revelations were, in fact, the fruit of a pact with the Devil. Like her, a Prioress of Lisbon repented in time, after years of painting her hands and feet with red ochre to simulate the stigmata.

With such an atmosphere, or, rather, miasma, floating over the entire country, a smoke shot red in places by the flames of the Inquisition, it was not surprising that the doors of the convents should be besieged by the daughters of both noble and humble houses. But here in the convent parlours a different temper prevailed. In many cases it was neither a desire for the religious life with all its implications nor a desire to obtain a transitory fame that urged the women of Spain towards the cloister. All too often, the convent was a comfortable refuge and a convenient social resort. Carmel has a stern name to-day, but Teresa trying to make up her mind to enter the Encarnacion had little real reason to dread a discipline too irksome for her pleasure-loving nature. She knew well enough that some came "solely to find a home." The Encarnacion was not a rich convent, but although the nuns had sometimes not enough to eat and could obtain leave to visit their relations in order to get a good meal, it was not grim at all, with its pleasant garden and its hospitable parlour (*locutorio*), warm red-bricked floors, and furniture of polished wood and leather. Worldly considerations were not entirely relinquished within its walls. Every nun was entitled to her private oratory in addition to her own cell, and if her fortune permitted was able to decorate it as she pleased, with paintings if her taste lay that way; she might also organise special celebrations nominally dedicated to the saint of her choice, but which in practice turned into little parties and concerts, giving the sisters an opportunity to show off their pretty voices. There was no obligation for a well-born girl to drop her worldly style and title; thus Teresa in the Encarnacion remained Doña Teresa de Ahumada as she had been in her father's palace. Personal bedizenment was not forbidden either; the nuns ornamented themselves with necklaces, bracelets, and rings, so incongruous with their habit that a contemporary writer exclaimed, "They adorn their persons like high-born ladies, forgetting that they are dead, that the cloister is a tomb, and that jewels are unbecoming to a corpse." The *locutorio* was the centre of social life. Friends and relations, both feminine and masculine, might be received there, and since everybody in the upper classes of a small city like Avila (its population numbered only about fourteen thousand souls all told), was related by a cat's cradle of interfamilial marriages to everybody else, there was no lack of gay young men to lounge in and out of the parlour under the convenient pretext of brotherhood or cousinship to some attractive inmate. Little presents changed hands, sweetmeats and oranges, jam, scent; and above all the novel produce of the New World, sweet potatoes, coffee, and even a drug from the Indies, reputed to possess medicinal properties of an unspecified nature. Many a sister had her little private store of provisions in reserve, to supplement the regulamentary diet. Gossip and the latest news circulated freely in that agreeable circle, called by Teresa "words of news and fribbles" (*vocablos de novedades y melingras*), and the fashionable topics of culture, philosophy, music, literature, and even, more dangerously, Platonic love, came under lively discussion during the long afternoons. Whether the freedom of life went further than mere talk must remain an open question; Teresa certainly thought it did, and she had every opportunity of judging it from the inside. Her own monastery was not very reprehensible, she said, and as for taking any liberty for herself, such as conversing through the door, or in secret, or by night, she did not think she could have brought herself to it and never did. But the phrase implies that others did, and she adds darkly that in other convents she had "seen and known."

It would seem also that novices were singularly ill-instructed in the history of their Order, for Teresa never knew until she found it out from a friend that the Rule had originally required of its members that they should possess nothing. Accustomed to the easy living of the Encarnacion, the idea of total poverty came as a surprise. Carmel had in fact deteriorated sadly in principles, manners, and performance since the first foundation which went back traditionally to the flanks of Mount Carmel in Lebanon. There, the prophet Elijah had abandoned his mantle to Elisha, having no further use for it, and had disappeared in a whirlwind up to Heaven. Following on this event, Elisha with a company of anchorites established themselves in the natural caves of that beautiful mountain, where, although chronologically long antecedent to the birth of Christ, they devoted themselves especially to the adoration of His Mother whose future existence had been miraculously revealed to Elijah. Bethlehem and Nazareth, indeed, lay not so very far away across the hills through the cedars and over the amazing carpet of wild flowers which in Elisha's day as in ours reappeared every spring to paint those lovely slopes in the colours of their maker. "There, living in small cells, like bee-hives, they made a sweet spiritual honey."

The anchorites taught not by the written word, but by example, and pilgrims came to profit by the society of the saintly men: a Greek inscription of the fourth century records it. It was not until the twelfth century, however, that a recognised community was mentioned by a Greek monk, Phocas (not to be confused with that charming saint and martyr, St. Phocas the Gardener), when he found a little chapel standing within a rampart, the centre of a true monastery whose members continued to lead their life of solitary contemplation in their separate caverns. By the end of the twelfth century the position on Mount Carmel had already become precarious; then the Saracens swept up to it after the fall of Acre (1291), burnt the buildings and massacred the hermits,—an incident damaging to the initial stronghold, but ultimately of value to the Order, which after this further disturbance of the hive began to swarm yet more freely towards the more hospitable lands of Europe. Cyprus, Sicily, France, and even distant England received the fugitives.* From these beginnings the monasteries spread quickly, especially in the university cities where seminarists were accepted to prepare for their academic honours. This development, though it served to extend the influence of Carmel, brought also the disadvantage of a confusion of purpose: the purely contemplative life and utter indigence of the mountain caves became modified under the touch of the world; the softness of deterioration set in, until in order to regularise the altered conditions it became necessary to ask the Pope's official sanction for a mitigation of the

* The exact places where the monks found refuge after their first migration in 1238 were Fortani in Cyprus, Messina in Sicily, Valenciennes and Aygalades near Marseilles in France. A second migration took place three years later, bound for England. They settled at Bradmer, in Norfolk, in the forest of Hulme, in Northumberland, and at Newenden and Aylesford, in Kent. Within a very few years (1249–1256) foundations were also established at Cambridge, Oxford, Paris, Bologna, York and Cologne.

original rule. Eugenius IV (1431–1447) complied; the vows of solitude and abstinence might be appreciably relaxed; one loosening led to another; and since the same thing was happening in the feminine Carmelite communities which had sprung up all over Europe after the advent of the masculine monasteries, the need for reform was apparent long before Teresa of Avila came to take it in hand. Such, in brief, were the successive steps leading up to her life-work. The demand was there for her to meet. But although Teresa, as a woman and a Carmelite, naturally confined herself to the establishment of reformed convents within that Order, it would be a mistake to suppose that so limited, so almost parochial a scope represented the true implications of her influence. By implication she was attacking the whole rot and demoralisation of the Spanish church, and the clergy knew it. She was doing something much more deep-reaching than to impose more stringent conditions upon a body of women too ready to take advantage of a mitigated rule. That she should put an end to the parties in the parlour, to the surreptitious notes passed through the gratings, to the little stocks of sweets in private cupboards, was of small account; that she should re-introduce the observance of true purity, true obedience, true poverty, and above all the enormous importance of God, was a great deal.

To the historian or theologian these reforms, in their complexity and endless knotted intrigues, may be of the most exquisite fascination, but to the less scholarly, less specialised student the more permanent interest lies in the personality of the woman who carried them out. This essay does not aspire to give the story of Teresa's foundations in any detail. The revision of Carmel and the establishment of seventeen new convents in Spain in the sixteenth century is not a subject which can hold a very general interest now. It is sufficient to say that no woman lacking the determination, the inspiration, and the ability of St. Teresa could possibly have triumphed. This visionary was one of the most capable women the world has seen. Not the least remarkable thing about her is the fact that nearly thirty years of life as an ordinary nun is not the best training or preparation for conflict with shrewd men, suspicious prelates, and jealous organisations, and the reader who chooses to pick his way through the tangle recorded in the documents is left wondering not only at the dissensions and treacheries of the men of God but also at the stature of the woman steering amongst them. One can accept her efficiency in the routine of administration; the authority she imposed on the Prioresses of her choice; the advice and regulations she issued in so firm a tone to her daughters; one can discover, with some amusement but not with excessive surprise, that the feminine details of daily life could receive her attention,—the most economical method of managing the laundry ("Your water-supply is excellent; Isabel might help Maria to wash,") the stockings which are to be made of cheap stuff; the cooking-stove which so took her fancy that she writes to her confessor about it, "A real treasure for all the friars and nuns . . . if you only read what they write about that stove you would not be surprised at these nuns wanting one like it." She was a born cook herself, they said, and all the nuns rejoiced when it came to her turn at the oven. Even when you were in the kitchen, she said, our Lord moved amidst the pots and pans. Her partiality for cleanliness had always been noted, and on one occasion brought her a reproof from a priest who on going to say Mass at one of her convents was given a scented towel to dry his fingers. He thought that such an abuse should be stopped and told her so, when "she answered me with charming grace, saying, 'Now, you must not be annoyed, for the nuns have learnt this defect from me.'" These things are not really to be wondered at. The wonder lay in her firmness, her skill in circumventing the traps of her enemies, her cool head, her powers of persuasion. She could talk round the General of the Order who had arrived full of hostility from Rome, but who ended by giving her everything she wanted. The Archbishop of Seville prevented her from kneeling to him and sank to his knees before her instead. Her own confessor was wont to say, "Good Lord, good Lord! I would rather argue with all the theologians in creation than with that woman." But that woman, who received the rare distinction of being made a Doctor of Theology, was also very much a woman of the world. Her aristocratic birth and upbringing counted for something, fitting her to meet her worldly compeers on equal terms. She completely disconcerted the high-born ladies of Madrid, who had crowded to see her in the expectation of elevated conversation, a possible miracle, and even a sudden onset of ecstasy. They were disappointed, for Teresa, instantly recognising the motive of their visit and their curiosity, would speak to them only in the most courteous and well-bred but entirely mundane language of the beauty of their own city, without the slightest allusion to the streets of the city of God.

E

XI

THE life of a nun belonging to a contemplative Order such as the Carmelite is commonly and correctly regarded as enclosed indeed, with a finality about it which brings the life-history to its conclusion save in matters relating to the soul. Spiritual progress is the only adventure left, but of that adventure the echoes are seldom likely to reach the outside world. Such, in fact, had been the fate of Teresa for nearly thirty years, and, since the Encarnacion had swallowed her up, there was no apparent reason why she should ever emerge or be heard of again. She had had her spiritual troubles, her tepidities, which had caused her to declare that on some days she found herself so destitute of courage as to be unable to kill an ant for God's sake if it made any resistance; she had had her inexplicable revelations of grace; but there was nothing unusual in all that, and a thousand parallel cases matched her own. It fell out, however, that when she had reached the age of fifty-seven, no longer a young woman, and a woman more-over whose health was constantly ravaged by the multiplicity of ailments from which she suffered, she entered suddenly upon a new stage of life, in which the quiet and obscurity of the monastery were to be exchanged for storm, notoriety, disputes, business, and an actual physical activity which would have taxed even a man in his prime.

Her first foundation was made at Avila itself, in a house which then became known as the convent of San José. Although the moment was ripe for such a foundation under reformed conditions, the inception of the idea came about almost accidentally in the course of conversation one night in Teresa's cell at the Encarnacion, when the discussion had turned on the absence of discipline and a girl exclaimed, "Well, let us who are here betake ourselves to a different and more solitary way of life, like hermits."

The venture raised an uproar in Avila, where it was said that Teresa was giving scandal and setting up novelties; the Governor and members of the Council assembled to declare that the new monastery was a wrong to the State and should not be allowed to exist; they even appointed delegates to protest legally; there was some talk of putting Teresa into prison; and all the inhabitants, she says, were so excited that they talked of nothing else. It was the topic of the day, but for all the outcry she cared little; it was only when Satan took a hand that she became distressed. He suggested to her that perhaps she had done wrong; that the nuns would not be content to live in so strict a house; that she herself, who was subject to so many infirmities, might not be able to bear so penitential a life, away from a large and pleasant house where she had so many friends; and finally that it was perhaps he himself who had contrived it in order to rob her of her peace and rest, so that, being unable to pray, she might be disquieted and lose her soul. These suggestions troubled her so much that she was "like one in the agony of death." The phrase is no exaggeration coming from the pen of one whose daily life was made up of such intensity of conviction. But not only was the whole human side of her nature now embattled by opposition, but of even greater degree than her capacity for being afflicted by the whispers of the Devil was her capacity for being sustained by the divine and secret reassurances of Christ.

Teresa spent five years at San José, which she describes as the most tranquil of her life. She may well have imagined that her days would end in those surroundings of the strictest austerity and poverty, imposed according to her own ideas, but, once embarked on her career of reform, she found it impossible to withdraw into a seclusion she perhaps only half desired in spite of her frequent declarations that she longed only to be alone. The duality of her nature, half active, half contemplative, came to disturb any settled existence, and after thirty-four years of convent life she took to the road, never again to leave it. In Medina del Campo, in Malagon, Valladolid, Toledo, Pastrana, Salamanca, Alba de Tormes, Segovia, Veas, Seville, Villanueva de la Jara, Palencia, Soria and Burgos, she successively descended from her creaking waggon and set about the establishment of yet another house of the Reform.* The foundation of San José had been tempestuous enough, but at least it had taken place within her own territory of Avila. Only when she started extending her activities to the other cities of Spain did she launch out on the series of journeys which took her up and down the difficult uncompromising country where the roads were often no better than rocky mountainous tracks and the climate varied between the heat of the sun and the furious winter's rages;

* Two other convents were founded in her absence, but under her guidance: that of Caravaca and that of Granada.

where the rivers were in flood, the inns verminous and revolting to a
woman of her fastidious nature; the population as likely to throw
stones as to kneel for her benediction; the muleteers and drivers
unreliable; the nuns who accompanied her terrified in adventures
where she alone could keep her head. Teresa, with her human side,
found it all very trying. "I felt a great dislike to journeys, especially
long ones"; and she peppers her writings with complaints and anecdotes that might come from the most secular pen, but for the pious
reflections which she throws in from time to time to the effect that
God may give us much to suffer for Him—"if only from fleas, ghosts,
and bad roads." A pity that unlike St. Bernard, *doctor mellifluus*, she
did not think of excommunicating the insects, so that they all died
as under his disapprobation in the church of Foigny.

They travelled usually in covered waggons with solid wooden
wheels and, of course, no springs. They were grateful for small
mercies. "The journey," writes Teresa, "was easier than when in a
two-wheeled cart." Such conveyances were still in such recent use in
Spain that Mrs. Cunninghame Graham, writing in the 1890's from an
intimate knowledge of the country, is able to give a picturesque but
accurate description: "Shut in on every side by the sackcloth awning,
the interstices carefully covered up with mats of esparto grass, with a
wooden crucifix and leather water-bottle hung up beside them, the
nuns travel all day long on the long and monotonous track, seeing
nothing of the landscape, hearing nothing but the tinkling of the bells
on the mules' collars, or the rough objurgations, the guttural '*arres!*'
of a muleteer. Perhaps through some little rent in the awning, invisible except to those within, a curious eye took a transient peep at
the world outside, but for the most part no details of changing landscape; of silvery olive-trees, their black stems rising against the brick-
coloured calcined earth; of foliage glittering in the sunlight; of waving
corn plain; of aromatic wastes covered with cistus thickets and lavender
and sage and all the sweet prickly family of savoury shrubs which
people these desolate upland wastes of uncultivated Castile; no glimpse
of fervid sky met the extinguished vision of the nuns, no free wind of
Heaven, no blast of sultry sun swept over their pallid faces, pallid with
the pallor of the cloister, and recalled them to the earth and sky. To
all this they were dead. At appointed times you might have heard,
were it not for the clatter of hoofs and the harness and the creaking

of the carts, the tinkling of a little bell, followed by a faint murmur from within—the sisters were saying Hours."

This caravan, swaying on its hooded way across the plains and over the hilly passes, accompanied by a miscellaneous retinue on horseback and mule-back, may have looked picturesque and even venerable in its traditional design, but romance is seldom what it seems, and the discomforts of this mode of travel were many. The heat in the carts was sometimes so great that "to go into them was like going into Purgatory." Teresa fell into a violent fever, but although they dashed water into her face, "it was so warm, because of the heat, that it gave me hardly any refreshment at all." The provisions they had taken with them, to last for several days, could not be eaten the following day. They had taken also a large pig-skin full of water, but so great was the scarcity of water that at a *venta* on the way the smallest jugful cost more than wine; and to make matters worse some perverse people set on one another with knives to the terror of the nuns, who were still inside the carts, the ground being too filthy for them to alight. At times they were glad to take their siesta in the shadow of a bridge, having first driven out the previous occupants, a herd of pigs. At other times they missed the road altogether, spending the whole day "in great toil, for the sun was very strong, and when we thought we were near the place we had to go as far again. I shall always," says Teresa, "remember that wearisome and winding road. We reached the house a little before nightfall, and the state it was in when we entered was such that we could not venture to pass the night there, because of the exceeding absence of cleanliness and the crowd of harvest men. The nun who was with me said to me, 'Certainly there is nobody, however great his spirituality, who could bear this; do not speak of it.' " This missing of the road was sometimes due to the ignorance of their guides, such as a young man who knew the way as far as Segovia but not by the high road, so led them into places where they frequently had to dismount, and even took the waggon over deep precipices where it almost swung into the air; sometimes to the sheer irresponsibility of the persons they had taken to show them the way, who would lead them so far as the roads were safe and would then leave them just before they came to a difficulty, saying that they had something to do elsewhere. Sometimes the roads were deep under water and the carts had to be dragged out of the mud, taking the mules out of one carriage to pull out the other, but frequently they suffered more than discomfort and inconvenience, and found themselves in actual danger. The carriage was often on the point of being overturned, especially when the drivers were young and careless. It happened also that the carriages must cross the Guadal-quiver by ferry, when "those who held the rope either let it go or lost it, and the boat went off with the carriages away from the rope and without oars." Fortunately, after swirling for some way down the swollen river they grounded on a sandbank, and a nobleman who had been looking down from a neighbouring castle compassionately sent people to their rescue. Teresa was once heard to observe that her sore throat and fever had prevented her adventures from amusing her as much as they should. She was, sometimes, very ill indeed on those expeditions, nor was there any comfort for the poor ageing invalid on arrival at her destination. They laid her on a bed, so uneven that it seemed made of sharp stones, in a small windowless room like a shed, and so hot that she decided to rise again and go on, for it seemed easier to bear the heat of the sun in the open country than in that little room. In bad weather, there was frequently no fire or fuel, and the roof was leaking to the rain. Even when she arrived at the house that was to be a new monastery she sometimes found that the friars, with more concern for the things of the spirit than for the things of the body, had made but little provision for the necessities of life; thus at Duruelo they had provided only hour-glasses, of which they had five, "and that amused me much." Yet her spirit was un-failing. They might lose their donkey, loaded with 500 ducats; they might find themselves suddenly in the midst of the bulls being driven in for next day's bull-fight; Teresa herself might become separated from her company, so that they ran in all directions, shouting for her through the night, ("Our loss," says Julian of Avila, a devoted but simple young priest who travelled with her, "was greater even than that of the donkey"); they might arrive to find lodging only in the granary of an inn that was too bad for them to enter, where a large salamander slipped up her arm beneath her tunic, still, although this time she "nearly died of fright," she preserved her vivacity and her charm. Even the muleteers and drivers, who refrained from their usual bad language in her presence, often said that nothing gave them so much pleasure as listening to her conversation; and as for her own travelling companions, she "put fresh life into us all with her excellent and most witty discourse, now giving utterance to things of great weight, now moving us to laughter. At other times she composed couplets," when something happened on the journey to furnish her with a theme. She certainly lived up to her own frequent exclamation, "God deliver me from sullen saints!"

XII

THE reformer and Foundress had no illusions at all on the subject of women in general or of nuns in particular. Her opinion of women's intellectual endowments was low. Their wits are dull; their foibles astonish even her at times; she knows by experience what women are when a number get together, and may God deliver us from it! She is "amused at your Reverence declaring that you could see her character at a glance," and assures him that women are not so easy to understand; he may hear their confessions for many a year and be astonished at the end to find how little he really knows about them. As for nuns, she knows that they do not shed their feminine weaknesses on taking the habit, and since it is with nuns that she is principally concerned, her scathing remarks occur *passim* throughout her writings. She has learned to mistrust them and their experiences; nor can you trust what they say, for if they want to do a thing they will find a thousand reasons for it, (*No se crea de monjas!*) It is not advisable to impose regulations in too much detail, since some sisters never come to an end of their scruples; thus, will Father Gracian please ordain that stockings may be either of coarse linen thread or worsted, and leave given to wear them; wimples, also, may be of linen instead of the prescribed hempen cloth. He might also abolish Father Pedro Hernandez' act forbidding the nuns to eat eggs or bread for their collation, as she does not want additions to the law of the Church which will make nuns over-scrupulous and harm them; at the same time, she takes the opportunity of reminding Father Gracian, in a broad hint, that Father Hernandez never made new regulations without telling her and discussing them with her first. Father Gracian and Father Mariano must be very wary indeed. Father Gracian is to attend to

what she says, and to believe that she understands women's whims
better than he does. Nuns tell tales against one another, and even
against their Prioress: this propensity must be checked. There is more
quiet and concord where nuns are few. Severity is strongly needed,
and although there may be an outcry for a few days most of the nuns
will be silent if they see that others are punished, for most women are
naturally timid. With tiresomeness or discontent she has of course no
patience. She knows what a discontented nun is, and dreads her more
than a host of devils. She would like to know what Sister Francisco means by the great strength she says God gives her, as she does
not explain it. How tiresome this is! Sister San Francisco gives way to
tears before the other nuns and they see her continually writing. That
which she writes is to be taken away and sent to Teresa. As for a nun
who has apparently gone out of her mind, perhaps she would leave
off screaming if she were to be slapped, and in any case it would do
her no harm. Some nuns have a mania for doing penances with
neither moderation nor discretion; this lasts two days, and then the
Devil makes them fancy that penance makes them ill. They fancy
that their head aches, and absent themselves from choir one day
because it aches, the next day because it has ached, and three more
lest it should ache again. Anything in the nature of showing off also
enraged her; excessive mortifications and demonstrations of piety
impressed her so little that it is difficult to credit the legend that she
once entered the refectory on all-fours, led on a rope by a sister, or
loaded her back with the panniers of a beast of burden. Grotesquely
suitable though the picture is to sixteenth-century Spain, it accords not
at all with the personality of Teresa. It is clear that she would stand no
nonsense, and in a fit of exasperation she writes to one of her Prioresses
that had two troublesome nuns been near her, Teresa, they would not
have undergone so many extraordinary experiences. Yet she did, oddly
enough, believe that many more graces were given to women than to
men, and at times she could relapse into a charming and maternal
tenderness, when she could remark that her nuns were so delighted
(with a change of house) that they seemed "just like little lizards
coming out into the sun in summer time."

That she was loved as well as feared is equally certain. In cold
weather—and it can be bitterly cold at Avila or Toledo—her daughters
would try to give her their own coverings for extra warmth. Some-

times, when they saw that she was tired, they would sing her to sleep. On other, more cheerful evenings, they would follow her to her cell and importune her to return to them for their entertainment. "Is your Reverence not coming to us?" and she answered laughingly, "Do you wish it, daughter? well, let us go together." Sometimes she played the tambourine and danced with them—an unexpected picture. There can be no doubt at all that Teresa was an exceptionally charming woman who inspired deep affection, which was sometimes sudden but always lasting; and that apart from her qualities of saintliness, apart even from the liveliness of her mind and the fascination of her conversation, the magnet which drew this response was her own warm humanity. It was all very well for her to preach a fine detachment from worldly affections: she did not, she could not, live up to her own precepts in the least. She fussed and worried unendingly over her brothers, their children, their marriages, their property, their law-suits, and, of course, their souls. But her anxieties were by no means confined to their souls. Her nephew Francisco is to marry Doña Orofrisia de Mendoza y de Castilla; she is related to the dukes of Albuquerque and Infantazgo, also to the marquises de las Navas and de Velada; no one in Spain comes of better blood; it is a highly satis-factory marriage (incidentally the bride is beautiful and very sensible), but what about the money due to Francisco from Peru? His brother must see about it immediately, or Francisco will not be able to main-tain his rank. Then there were her friends, both secular and religious; an astonishing number. Reading her letters, or her own history of her Foundations, she seems to be perpetually picking up new people and attaching them to herself. How she found time for them all, with the innumerable things she had to do, remains a wonder; she founded seventeen convents in less than twenty years, contending with the most complicated difficulties, settling and directing every detail; she was concerned in the foundation of a number of monasteries for friars as well; she undertook those long, fatiguing, and often dangerous journeys all over Spain; she wrote a quantity of books; she suffered from the interruption of constant illness; yet the letters continue to pour out in a torrent, intimate, affectionate, upbraiding, practical, dashing from subject to subject, breathless, ("Alas, I ought to write with both hands in order not to omit one subject for another;") she hopes she will manage to write a short letter this time, but she never does; they flow on and on, in a large hand on single open sheets, folded and sealed afterwards with one of her two seals, the monogram J.H.S. or a skull, (but as she did not like the skull, her brother must send the other one, "for I cannot endure this death's head;") the spelling is phonetic, punctuation totally disregarded save for an occasional upright line in place of a full-stop, so that the whole letter reads as a single sentence and the recipient sometimes had to use his own discretion in interpreting what the saint really meant. "I never revise my letters," she writes; "if any letters in the words are missing, fill them in. One sees at once what the words are meant for and it would be loss of time to correct them." She is particular about her pens: her nephew must send her some well-cut ones, for she has changed pens so many times during the course of the letter that the handwriting will look worse than usual but "much to my disgust and trouble" there are none to be got in Toledo. Sometimes she employs a secretary, whose task must have been as alarming as it was inspiring, for Teresa much disliked not writing to her friends herself and also we may suppose that her mind worked quite as rapidly in dictation as in transcribing by her own hand. One is not surprised to hear that one of these secretaries "stands in great need of prayer," or that another one, in understandable haste, learns to write by a miracle, after being told to copy one of Teresa's letters.

Her correspondents do not have an easy time either, and one surmises that the arrival of the courier bearing one of her enormous missives produced an anxious as well as a pleasurable flutter. For one thing, the letter must be answered, and answered quickly, in detail, and legibly. Whatever Teresa's own handwriting might be like she insisted that any report should be "clearly written so that I am not obliged to copy it out." Exaggerations, also, are intolerable; the writer may think that her rhodomontades are not falsehoods, but such a style is far from perfect; let her write frankly, and amend her style, and not spin out her letters, and then Teresa will be satisfied with her. But what really arouses her wrath is to get no reply at all. Has Fray Antonio taken a vow not to answer her letters? She will not write to him again, for it seems that she might as well talk to a deaf-mute. As for Father Gracian, "Oh, God help me, what a provoking character you have! I declare I must be very virtuous to write to you, and the worst of it is that you are infecting the Licentiate Padilla, for, like you, he neither writes nor sends me any news of himself. God forgive you both! When I consider the difficulties you have left me in and how forgetful you are of everything, I do not know what to think except 'Cursed is the man that puts his trust in man.' " Surely somewhat unusual language for a nun to use to her confessor. And it is not only the dilatoriness of her correspondents which brings them a scolding. The long-suffering Father Gracian is constantly getting into trouble. He is informed that his letter would have been capital had he left Latin quotations alone. Then she is very much annoyed that he should have gone away into Andalusia, leaving her at Burgos. Fray Mariano too, she cannot understand why he has not sent a reply by the carter, nor can she understand what he is doing in Madrid and why he is not staying with the Mitigated friars. He is not to argue with the Archbishop; and he is to speak with restraint when he has to complain of anyone, for she fears he is careless, being so extremely frank. The Father Provincial of the Company of Jesus receives an answer couched in terms of such indignation that he is obliged to beg her to read his letter again, when her feelings have subsided; then she may take it in a kindlier way. Her reply shows, however, that she was not in the least mollified. Her Prioresses fare no better. Mother Mary of St. Joseph is informed that Teresa would have considered it a piece of good fortune if she could have managed to pass through Seville in order to scold her to her heart's content. The Prioress at Valladolid is reminded that she is "a very insignificant person in yourself." The Prioress at Granada receives a letter (it occupies eight pages of print) of such violent castigation that it almost produces a sense of vicarious guilt in the modern reader. Nor was her severity inadvertent, or the result of dashing off her epistles at top speed with an overheated pen, for more than once she remarks quite complacently that she has written "terrible things" and wonders whether her correspondent will ever speak to her again. No wonder that a harassed Corregidor was driven finally into saying, "Let it be done at once. In spite of ourselves, we are all obliged to do whatever she wants."

The tone she sometimes adopts towards the All-Highest is startlingly similar, for, like all people of strong personality, her accent is always unmistakeable; her utterances always in her own authentic voice. In this she resembled say Dr. Johnson or the Duke of Wellington. Is she indeed addressing God, or some recalcitrant friar? Hear her speak.

Charged by our Lord with a message to deliver to a certain person, a type of mission she particularly disliked, she retorted, "Why dost Thou give me this trouble? Canst Thou not speak directly to that person?" On another occasion she was heard on a river-bank informing God that the reason He had so few friends was that He treated them so badly, a theory which seemed fixed in her mind, for she writes also to Father Gracian saying that although "God treats His friends terribly, He does them no wrong for He served His Son in the same way."

But when she chose to be affectionate, how gracious she could be! At those times she must surely have been forgiven all the lashes of the whip she could coil round the wincing body of her victims. Of her deliberate compliments it was said that she always put a grain of pepper into them, but when no compliment was intended, and nothing but her warm heart overflowed, there was no pepper, no sting, nothing but the spontaneity of love like the caressing sun. There was something truly maternal and protective about Teresa in her personal relationships. No detail concerning her friends was too small to arouse her interest and concern. She is extremely worried to hear that Father Gracian has fallen off his mule; she does not know what sort of a mount it is, nor why he thinks it necessary to travel ten leagues a day, which on a pack-saddle is enough to kill him; but in any case she thinks he ought to be strapped on to prevent his tumbles. God grant his fall has not injured him! And has it occurred to him to wear more clothes now that the weather is cold? Five years later she is still worrying about his mount; she is afraid the little mule is not suited to him, though, indeed, she is not so frightened of his falling off the little mule as off a larger animal which might unseat him. Still, she thinks it would be well for him to buy a good one. She sends him a bezoar stone to wear round his neck, as an antidote against poison. When he leaves her at Palencia she sends a letter after him, asking if he does not see how short a time her happiness has lasted; she had hoped to undertake her next journey in his company, but "O my Father! thank God for having given you such charming manners that no one else seems to fill your place." She can tease him too, but gently: "Whenever I recall your words I am amused at the solemn manner in which you declared that I must not judge my superior. O my Father, how little need there was for you to swear, even like a saint much less like a muleteer. . . ." Father Gracian was perhaps her favourite,—early in their acquaintance she had written that he was perfect in her eyes,— but others had their share of her attention. She is extremely sorry that Father Mariano is so delicate; Father Gracian must see to it that he eats well, and must on no account allow him to go to Rome until he is stronger. Don Francisco de Salcedo must not repeat so often that he is growing old, for it cuts her to the heart. Mother Mary of St. Joseph, the one who escaped a verbal scolding, receives sudden messages which must have provided a more than adequate compensation: "I cannot tell you why I love you so much. . . . I assure you that if you love me dearly, I love you in return and like to hear you tell me so. How natural it is to us to wish for a return!" How natural indeed; but the exclamation comes somewhat unexpectedly from one whom we have been taught to regard as an austere and other-worldly visionary. This same visionary is concerned about Mother Mary's clothing; how foolish she is to wear a woollen tunic in summer! She will please take it off directly she receives this letter. Nor can the saint rise superior to a rather childish greediness. She hopes that Father Gracian will not forget to send her her Easter cake,—the equivalent of our Easter egg, it was made of eggs baked in dough. As for the butter that a friend has sent her, it tasted very nice, and she will accept it on condition that she may be given some more when it is particularly fine. The quinces which came with the butter were delicious too. She hears that the *aloja* (a kind of metheglin, or spiced mead) is very good at Valladolid, but fears she will not get any. And there are constant references to sweets, sardines, partridges, radishes, lettuces, apples, orange-flower water; all gifts which had a special value in the eyes of one who had renounced her birthright of good-living in exchange for the utmost poverty, and whose diet moreover was frequently insufficient. Teresa had been born with a liking for agreeable things, and although her vow forbade them she was far too human ever to turn herself into a sour and disapproving ascetic. Works of art appealed to her; she is "delighted with the charming things sent for the Administrator"; the small goblet is the daintiest she ever saw, and she can see no harm in his drinking from such a graceful little tankard, although his habit is of serge. Conversely, she aptly remarks that a *patio* at Seville looks as though it were built of iced sugar; those who have seen some *patios* in Seville will know how true the description is. In spite of her appreciation, however, she was some-times a little casual; she does not know why the two emerald rings and the large *Agnus Dei* cannot be found; she cannot remember where she put them, nor whether they were ever handed to her at all. . . .

One of the most charming aspects of Teresa's nature is revealed through her relationship with children. Reading through her letters, one get the impression that a lot of little girls were always clinging round her skirts. There were Elenita and Isabelita and Teresita, and whenever the saint writes about them she does so with the amused indulgence of a favourite aunt or grandmother. The note which then comes into her letters is gay, tender, and good-humoured indeed. To Elenita, whom she calls "my little chubby," (*mi gordilla*,) she sends a joking message, "Tell my Elena not to stay away from me." Immedi-ately the child threw on her cloak and started off. "Hola, senora?" her mother cried, "is that the way girls leave their mother's house?" "The Mother Foundress has sent for me," Elena replied. "I can do no less."

Isabelita, who was Father Gracian's little sister, aged ten, evidently filled Teresa's life with delight. Busy woman and great saint though she was, she could unbend entirely in the rare moments she was able to find for "this Bela of mine," and the little childish anecdotes come with evident pleasure from her pen even in the midst of the most serious matters. "The other day, when I gave her a piece of melon, she declared it was so cold it froze her throat. She says the quaintest things and is always merry. . . . The little creature's wits are extraordinary. There is only one thing about her that troubles me. I do not know how to manage her mouth, which is very prim; she laughs very primly too, yet she is always laughing. Sometimes I tell her to open it, some-times to shut it, and sometimes not to laugh. She says it is not her fault but the fault of her mouth, which is true. Anyone who has seen her wishes to see her again, though I do not tell her so. You would be amused to see the life I lead her about the expression of her mouth. I think it will not be so prim when she grows older." But alas, although "she affords me the greatest amusement, I have so much writing to get through that I can spend but little time with her." In such little time as Teresa was able to give her, however, she managed to win the child's devotion even as she won the devotion of everybody else.

Isabelita made up a verse which she sang whenever Teresa appeared
at recreation:

> Oh see to recreation
> The Mother Foundress enter!
> Then let us dance and sing her songs
> With music to content her.

An imaginative little inmate of the Toledo convent. Teresa gives also
a sketch of her at play: "She has a few poor little statues of some
shepherds, some nuns, and a figure of our Lady, and not a feast-day
comes round but she invents some little scene with them; she composes
verses, and sings them to us so well and to such a pretty tune that we
are astonished."

These flitting children were the gaiety of the monasteries and their
foundress. Teresita, aged eight, was Teresa's own niece, given into
her care as soon as she reached Spain from the New World. "She seems
the sprite of the house and knows how to amuse us, telling us about
the Indians and the sea voyage better than I could. . . . You are more
just than Teresita who approves of no one but the sisters at Seville. . . .
She is not writing to you because she is busy: she says she is Prioress
and sends you her love." By such touches, which she little thought
would survive and glisten into a distant century, she registers no less
actually than a painter the intimate scenes with the confiding children
grouped round her in the centre.

XIII

It seems somewhat hard that Teresa, as a consequence of undertaking
those trying journeys, should have been described by an angry Papal
Nuncio as a restless gad-about (*femina inquieta, andariega*). "Do not
mention her name!" he exclaimed, continuing with a fine indignant
rhetoric, "She is a disobedient contumacious woman who promulgates
pernicious doctrine under the pretence of devotion; leaves her cloister
against the orders of her superiors and the decrees of the Council of
Trent; is ambitious and teaches theology as though she were a doctor
of the Church, in contempt of the teaching of St. Paul who com-

manded women not to teach." Teresa, secure in her conviction that her work of reform needed doing and aware also that she had proceeded most cautiously with the proper authorisations, received all such assaults with calm. "I am amused at the plan of sending me to the Indies," she wrote on hearing that the Mitigated friars were plotting to get rid of her by those means; "God forgive those people! However, it is best for them to make so many accusations at once, as no one will believe them." She was quite alive to the fact that she herself had produced all the turmoil, remarking that she heartily regrets being a stumbling-block and thinks that the best remedy might be to throw her, like Jonah, into the sea, but so long as she did nothing against her own conscience, or against her most sacred vow of obedience, she could sail undisturbed over the stormiest waves.

In the very midst of her occupations and difficulties she received instructions to return to Avila, there to become Prioress of her own convent of the Encarnacion. The convent had gone from bad to worse, and now provided nothing but a dismal example of how necessary her Reform had been. Teresa was most reluctant to accept this office, and even wrote to her friends there asking them not to vote for her, for she was anxious to continue with her own work which she saw would be seriously interrupted by three years' detention at Avila, but Christ spoke to her, saying that it was His will. Unfortunately the nuns of the Encarnacion remained uninitiated to the divine intention, and Teresa's reception was turbulent to a degree. Humanly speaking, one must have a certain sympathy with the self-indulgent community: Teresa's departure from their midst had been in itself a criticism of their way of life, the establishment of the Reformed houses had carried that criticism further, and now to cap all they saw themselves threatened with the very rule that had so disquieted them. When the Provincial, accompanied by Teresa, entered the choir and read the letters patent confirming her appointment, he was met by an outcry from the mob of shrieking and hysterical women. Some of them even fainted, so great was their resentment and emotion. Teresa took a calm control. Apologising to them for her unwelcome arrival, and expressing her sense of her own unworthiness, she silenced them for the moment and later addressed them in words full of dignity, firmness, and conciliation. "My sisters, our Lord has sent me to this house to undertake this post by reason of my obedience, one which I as little expected as deserved. This election has given me great distress, not only because it has forced on me duties that I may not be able to fulfil, but also because it has given you a Prioress against your will and taste. I come only to serve you, and to administer to your pleasure so far as I am able. There is no reason to dread one who is so entirely yours. Do not fear my rule, for although I have lived until now and ruled amongst Discalced nuns, I know well enough how those who are not should be governed." The visionary certainly knew how to deal with human beings, and before very long the subdued sisters were offering her the keys of their own accord. When more serious troubles came upon her, and she found herself threatened by the Inquisition itself, she accepted the situation boldly and without discomfiture. Her friends in alarm tried to frighten her; they came to her saying that the times were dangerous, that something might be laid to her charge, that she might be taken before the Inquisitors. Teresa "heard this with pleasure, and it made me laugh because I never was afraid of them. I knew well enough that in matters of faith I would not break the least ceremony of the Church, and that I would expose myself to die a thousand times rather than that anyone should see me go against it or against any truth of Holy Writ. So I told them I was not afraid of that, for my soul must be in a very bad state if there was anything the matter with it of such a nature as to make me fear the Inquisition." This was her invariable attitude. On one occasion a rebellious novice, anxious to quit the convent in Seville, denounced the nuns with accusations of heresy, and poor Father Gracian going to visit Teresa was terrified to see the carts of the Inquisition waiting to take away the nuns, while their officers were searching the convent and a priest was watching from the corner of the street. Teresa only laughed, saying "Well and good, Father! let them burn us all for Christ's sake, but never fear lest any of us should err from the faith, for by God's grace we would sooner die a thousand times." Not content with reassuring her friends, she went off to find the Inquisitor in person, and informed him that although she was subject to certain extraordinary processes in prayer, such as ecstasies, raptures and revelations, she did not wish to be deluded or deceived by Satan or to do anything that was not absolutely safe. Sooner than that, she would give herself up to the Inquisition for them to try her and examine her ways of going on. It was in

F

reply to this declaration that the Inquisitor commanded her to write the history of her life, and to submit it, not to the Inquisition, but to a priest known as the Apostle of Andalusia. In justice to the Inquisition, this command may be signalled as an example of their genuine desire to protect rather than to persecute souls against the mortal peril of heresy. The Inquisitor made no attempt to destroy Teresa; he merely put her on the road to find out for herself whether her "extraordinary processes" proceeded from Heaven or from Hell. She must have felt grateful to him, for it was a subject which owing to the bewilderment and spiritual incompetence of her confessors in the past had always much troubled her.

It will probably never be known beyond doubt whether the Princess of Eboli was really responsible for bringing a copy of Teresa's autobiography into the hands of the Inquisition. It is certain that backed by her husband, the attractive Ruy Gomez, she importuned the reluctant Teresa into giving her a copy, under promise of secrecy, but within a few days Teresa heard that the promise had been broken, the book had been left lying about, the servants' had got hold of it, her revelations were a matter of common talk and jest, she was being compared with the fraudulent Magdalen of the Cross, and was the subject of gossip in the drawing-rooms of Madrid. This was vexatious enough, but fortunately it had no serious consequences, for although the Inquisition eventually obtained a copy, sent directly, it is said, by the Princess, with a denunciation of its dangerous doctrines, the report given on it by a Dominican friar appointed as censor was so favourable to Teresa, that in the end the episode did her more good than harm. She was declared no deceiver, and the dozen convents of barefooted nuns which she had already founded were pronounced models of austerity and perfection. Further, the Cardinal-Archbishop of Toledo, President of the Supreme Court of the Inquisition, received her warmly, saying that he was glad to see her, had read the book himself, regarded it as containing sound and wholesome doctrine, and would grant her the licence she then required for a new foundation. Teresa had triumphed. The manuscript of that controversial book, in her own handwriting with few erasures, no punctuation, no division into paragraphs, and no title, on yellowed paper bearing the water-mark of Valladolid and Salamanca, now lies bound in crimson velvet by order of Philip II in the innermost sanctuary of the Escorial.

XIV

THIS Princess of Eboli was only one of the strange characters that populated Teresa's life. The saint's range of acquaintance was extensive, partly thanks to her faculty for acquiring friends and retaining them; partly to her own noble birth which enabled her to consort on easy terms with the proudest names in Spain; partly to her profession and the activities connected with her Reform, which brought her into touch with Cardinals, Archbishops, and other high dignitaries of the Church, as well as with the most ragged of friars. She wrote frequently to the King, to whom she used to refer as "my friend the King," and met him personally when after their interview he made her "the most courteous bow I ever saw."* With the Duke and Duchess of Alba she was on really intimate terms, interested in every matter connected with their family life, and sometimes their guest in their castle above the river Tormes on her way to Salamanca. The contrast between the ducal castle and the dirty lodgings of the wayside inns, which were her usual lot, may strike us as forcibly as it struck Teresa herself. Fond though she was of the duchess and that great soldier her husband, she did not wholly approve of their establishment. "Imagine," she wrote, "that you are in an apartment,—I fancy it is termed a private museum,—belonging to a king or great nobleman, in which are placed numberless kinds of articles of glass, porcelain, and other things, so arranged that most of them are seen at once on entering the room. While on a visit to the Duchess of Alba I was taken into such a room. I stood amazed on entering it and wondered what could be the use

---

* It is amusing to note, considering the difference in their positions as the most dreaded monarch of Christendom and the plain nun, that Philip rather than Teresa had in the first instance been the suppliant for a meeting. On her way through Madrid she had given his sister a letter for him, relating some advice received by her from God in connexion with his most secret thoughts. So struck by this letter was Philip, that he exclaimed, "Why can I not see this woman? where is she?" But Teresa had already left for Toledo, and he had to wait eight years before she came. Then it was only because she wanted to ask a favour, which he immediately granted, after inquiring whether that was all she desired. Characteristically, she then dictated the terms of her petition in her own words to the Duke of Alba's secretary.

Tradition says that she boldly opened her remarks to Philip by saying, "Sire, you are thinking, 'I see before me this gad-about woman,'" the description which had been given of her by the Papal Nuncio.

of such a jumble of knick-knacks. Although I was in the room some time, there were so many things in it that I forgot what I had seen and could no more remember each object, nor of what it was made, than if I had never seen it, though I recalled the sight of the whole collection," observations which she did not fail to turn to a cautionary illustrative purpose. Looking through the volumes of her letters, the noble names recur: Alba, Medina-Celi, Mendoza, Braganza. . . .

But the Princess of Eboli was a thorn in Teresa's side. This violent, spoilt, unreliable, beautiful woman, with the black patch worn always over a blinded eye, credited with many lovers who were said to include the King, threw Teresa's convent of Pastrana into consternation by rushing there "in the tumult of her grief for her husband's death." Teresa herself was not there at the time, but the Prioress, awakened at two in the morning with the news that the princess was on her way, exclaimed, "The princess a nun? Then I give up this house for lost." As it was too late to stop her, if indeed anybody could have succeeded in doing so, she presently arrived in a cart, having in an excess of mortification refused to travel in her own coach, and proceeded to fling the convent into confusion. She had already provided herself with a Carmelite habit, so dirty that the nuns hastened to give her a clean one; she now insisted that two women she had brought with her should be given the habit likewise and should be admitted as novices. On the Prioress protesting that such a thing was not to be done without the sanction of the Superior, the princess (who had, in fact, been the main benefactress of the foundation) cried out in a fury, "What have the friars to do with my monastery?" It had begun ill, and continued worse. Her behaviour was wildly contradictory; on the one hand she insisted on humiliating herself into the lowest place in the refectory, but on the other hand she compelled the nuns to serve her on their knees and salute her by her titles; demanded that her own maids should wait on her, received her friends and their retinues, in complete disregard for the rules of the reformed Order; and, on this being objected to, removed herself in a rage to one of the hermitages in the garden, had a door cut in the wall, and received her friends there, to the great indignation and distress of the nuns, who saw their privacy outraged and yet, in their gratitude, tried to remember the benefactions their house had once received at the princess's hands. But now, worst of all, those benefactions were withdrawn. The princess, who was beginning to recover from her grief and also perhaps to regret her impulse, removed herself altogether to her own palace within the walls of Pastrana and suppressed the allowance hitherto made to the necessitous community, leaving it to struggle on or to starve as best it might.

They appealed to Teresa, who after some abortive negotiations with the princess, acted with her customary decision. It was not in her nature to continue for long as a suppliant on unwilling charity. Orders came from her that the convent should be abandoned, and in spite of the attempted interference of the princess, who threatened to place guards at the gates and also sent a messenger "to say many things," the nuns, accompanied by priests and friars, secretly took their departure at midnight in five carts for the protective comfort of Teresa and the refuge of Segovia.

It was typical of Teresa's Spain that an erratic and worldly intriguer like the Princess of Eboli should, in the first place, wish to endow a convent, and, in the second, rush to it as an inmate the moment she found herself in distress, for religion and the worldly life were confusingly intermingled. Fortunately, other figures of a very different stamp moved also within the periphery of the saint. To turn from the gusty episode of the Princess of Eboli, to turn even from the cabals, factions and suspicions of the Church, from the sordid difficulties with which Teresa so continuously had to cope, from the hysterical immolations and mortifications of pious persons with their sores and sackcloth, to the serene purity of a St. John of the Cross, is like moving from a bewildering storm into the heavenly calm where it is light and the birds sing. Teresa's Spain, abounding also in deplorable examples of religious fervour gone wrong, ripened a rare vintage of distilled holiness when all the imagination of that otherwise unimaginative race passed into the mysticism which has been called the natural produce of the Spanish soil. Among her countrymen and contemporaries she could number St. Peter of Alcantara, St. Ignatius Loyola, St. Thomas of Villanueva, St. Louis Bertrand, St. Francis Borgia, the "duke turned Jesuit"; the eloquent Juan de Avila, Apostle of Andalusia; Luis de Granada, preacher and writer; Luis Ponce de Leon; and the loveliest spirit of all, Juan de Yepez, known to Teresa as Fray Juan de la Cruz, to us as St. John of the Cross.

Among the crowd of friars, confessors, prioresses, nuns, princes, and ladies who pullulate with such actuality through the records of Teresa's life, St. John for all his elusiveness shines with a light of his own. We never seize him; he possessed more than any man the *pudeur* of suppressing his own personality. He is an essence, volatile, imponderable, floating in a rarefied atmosphere difficult for us to breathe, his one desire to pass unnoticed, the better to lose himself in the only preoccupation which held any significance for him. Like the ideal soul of which he writes, he is "free, perfect, solitary, and pure." Free indeed; for he had divorced himself from all attachments, "such as to individuals, to a book or a call, to a particular food, to certain society, to the satisfaction of one's taste for science, news, and such things." Does it make any difference, he asks, whether a bird be held by a slender thread or a rope since it is bound and cannot fly until the cord that holds it be broken? the solitary bird which can endure no companionship, even of its own kind. He himself had broken all bonds:

> Forth unobserved I went
> In darkness and security,
> By the secret ladder, in disguise,
> In secret, seen of none,
> Oh night more lovely than the dawn!
> Lost to all things and myself,
> And, amid the lilies forgotten,
> Threw all my cares away.

This poet, this mystic, this wholly unpractical being, emptied into a sublime lack of interest in anything topical or transitory, was sometimes obliged to strike the wall with his fist, to being himself back through that small sharp pain to reality.

Teresa, of course, with her quick perception of character, realised that she could make no use of him as she could make of her other friars; he could not be sent on errands or charged with the execution of anything regarding organisation. She may have tried, without success; for although she does not enlarge on the reason for her vexation, she does remark that she was "vexed with him at times." Nor does she, who was nevertheless observant and capable of giving such vivid descriptions as, say, her description of St. Peter of Alcantara who resembled the roots of trees, ever attempt to bring the physical presence of St. John before the eyes of her readers. Her reticence sug-

gests an intuitive recognition of the unimportance of corporal clothing
to such a spirit. She notes only that he was very small, "small in stature
but great in God's sight," and one of her favourite jokes was to say
that she had got a friar and a half—the other being a man of particularly
imposing stature. But she also realised, and at first sight, that here was
a man she needed to attach to herself and her Reform. At their very
first meeting, in fact, which she had contrived with some difficulty
owing to his reluctance to speak with women, she argued him out
of his intention to desert the Carmelite Order in favour of the Car-
thusians. She knew him at once for what he was, as he, no doubt,
was equally impressed by her own quality at this coming together of
the two great mystics of Spain, whose names can never be divided.

It would be misleading to suggest that she made no use of him at
all, for she did install him as confessor and spiritual director at the
Encarnacion when she was made Prioress of that convent. But this
was an employment for which his spiritual qualifications, in which
she had great faith, especially suited him—a very different matter
from the tasks she was apt to exact of her other adherents. It would
be misleading also to suggest that St. John played no part in active
life, since he did hold certain offices at various times and even became
Vicar for Andalusia, a position he cannot have relished since his dislike
of the people of that province equalled Teresa's own—"he cannot,"
she writes, "bear the Andalusians." Yet, in spite of these responsi-
bilities imposed upon him by exterior circumstances, in spite even of
the "solid judgment" with which Teresa credited him, one cannot
feel that St. John's association with affairs was anything but
fortuitous.

Austere and ascetic, St. John "amid the lilies forgotten," is far too
delicate, exquisite, and poetical a wisp ever to be associated with
the intrigues of men, nor, blessedly, with the frequent grimness
of religion. Neither he nor Teresa was grim, but for her part this
welcome lack may be attributed to her humour, humanity, and robust-
ness of outlook; for his, to a certain fragrance and diaphaneity which
seem to envelop his whole slight being. "The first of the passions of
the soul and the will," he writes, "is joy"; and he might be writing
of himself when he goes on to depict one who, pure in heart, has
found in all things that knowledge of God which is delicious, sweet,
chaste, pure, spiritual, joyous, and loving (*gozosa, gustosa, casta, pura,*

espiritual, alegre y amorosa). It comes with no surprise to find him singing to himself along the road, or sitting by night in a meadow near a running brook, gently discoursing—for this time he had a companion—on the beauty of the sky, the moon and the stars (*la hermosura del cielo, luna y estrellas*) and the sweet harmony in the movements of the heavens (*la dulce harmonia que hacen los cielos con sus movimientos*). There was even an element of pantheism in him, which led him to practise his orisons in the closest touch with nature, spending the whole night in a wood or kneeling among the reeds by a stream. Water he loved, especially running water, as Teresa loved it; water, and rocks, and trees, with a fervour more compatible with the poet in him than with the saint who was the supreme preacher of detachment from everything but God.

For with St. John of the Cross, even more than with St. Teresa, we are moving on planes of the most complete abstraction. He is striving, through the inadequate medium of language, to express something which he knows to be essentially unexpressible. No one is to be surprised, he says, on finding his book somewhat obscure, for only he who has passed through the trials of the soul can know them, but even then he cannot explain them. But, far more of a poet than she, he employs symbolism to an even greater extent; it seems, indeed, that his use of this device is not so much deliberate, as natural to him; it is the very idiom and mould of his mind. Above all things the poet of night, he discriminates to a hair-splitting nicety between the varying degrees of darkness. To be in obscurity (*estar a oscuras*) is for instance different in degree from being in utter darkness (*estar en tinieblas*), and the fading of night into dawn is for him a fine dividing thread of change to be recorded with the utmost delicacy (*como la noche junto ya a los levantes de la mañana*). So great and instinctive is his power of identification between the thought and the symbol, that the one slides by a natural transition into *becoming* the other; thus, speaking of fire in the night, it is the night itself which becomes the fire, not the fire which is added to the night—the kind of image which constantly haunted St. John, to whom, by a curious reversal of ordinary notions, the profoundest darkness could grow luminous by virtue of its own obscurity. In the same spirit he could write of lovers in a lovely strophe,

i Oh noche che guiaste,
    Oh noche amable mas que la alborada,
    Oh noche que juntaste
    Amado con amada,
    Amada en el amado transformada!

    (Oh night which teaches,
    Oh night more delightful·than dawn,
    Oh night which joins
    The lover to the beloved,
    The beloved into the lover transformed!)

It is logical, it is inferential, that "the All contained in the Nothing," which is the summing up of his philosophy, should appear as a perfectly easy concept to a metaphysician whose mind worked innately in such a way.

XV

TERESA was growing old; she was stout now; her speech had become indistinct, and she walked leaning always on the crooked ebony staff her brother had brought her from the Indies. Her skin was "the colour of earth"; her teeth black with decay; and stiff hairs now sprouted from the three moles which had once been thought to add piquancy to her face. Her left arm, which the Devil had broken by throwing her down a flight of stairs one Christmas-eve, and which had had to be re-broken and re-set most painfully several times, was almost useless to her, since although she could lift it to her head and could move the hand, she was quite unable to dress or undress herself or even to adjust her veil. Before she was sixty she was already describing herself as old and worn out, but by the time she is sixty-seven, and not far off her death, she is "aged and feeble, good for little now, very old and weary, though my desires are still vigorous." But at least she had lived to witness a great belated triumph: the granting of a decree which after all those years of struggle recognised the Reform and allowed its members to serve God unmolested according to their lights. Philip II had always been favourable to Teresa and her associates, and this was his crowning effort on their behalf. "None but He alone who knows the labours that have been suffered," wrote Teresa; "the twenty-five years of trials and persecutions and afflictions I have passed through, can understand the joy that came to my heart." She had much to be thankful for in her reward. Her reputation stood high among her countrymen, and the crowd of those anxious to receive her blessing sometimes made it difficult for her to descend from her cart. Still, gratifying though all this might be, there was to be no rest for the old woman, much as she longed for it. She was, as usual, on her travels when news reached her at Medina del Campo that the Duchess of Alba urgently desired her presence during the confinement of her young daughter-in-law, the Duchess of Huescar, and had, in fact, sent her own coach to fetch her. Teresa's last journey was thus not made in a waggon, but in one of the few coaches then existent in Spain,—there were not more than four or five in the whole country,—resplendent with the armorial bearings of the great house of Alba. A faithful and much-tried companion went with her, Anna of St. Bartholomew, she who had miraculously learned to write in order to serve Teresa as her secretary as well as her infirmarian, and who has left a most detailed and moving account of this their last expedition together. Teresa set out from Medina in sad circumstances: having had occasion to rebuke the Prioress for some trifling lapse, she was answered in a manner which she considered to be insubordinate and undutiful; this so distressed her that she could eat nothing and was unable to sleep all night. They had taken nothing with them to eat on the road, surely a reprehensible omission on the part of Anna, nor could they buy anything on the way, not even in a poor village, Peñaranda de Bracamonte, where they were compelled to spend the night. Teresa by now was exceedingly weak and suffering from fever; "Daughter," she said, "give me something for I am fainting," but Anna had only some dried figs, and although she offered four *reals* for some eggs, not caring what they might cost, the money was brought back to her as there was nothing to be had in the village. She never could describe, she said, what affliction she was in then; it seemed to her as if her heart were broken, and she could not look at the saint without weeping, for her face seemed half dead. Teresa with her true kindness tried to comfort her, saying that the figs were very good and that there were many poor people who did not get such a treat.

The next day, in another village, they managed to get some herbs boiled with onions, and that was all they had until they reached Alba de Tormes in the evening. Ironically enough, after their haste and privations, a messenger met them with the information that the young duchess had been safely delivered. "Thank God," said Teresa, whose humour never deserted her, "this saint will no longer be needed."

She did not lodge in the ducal castle where she had noticed the room piled with such a jumble of knick-knacks, but in her own convent in the heart of the town, overlooking the river and the plain beyond. Here she received treatment very different from Medina del Campo. The loving welcome and solicitude of her daughters touched her deeply. She seems to have been softened by illness and exhaustion, for she allowed them to kiss her hand, a thing she generally discouraged; used endearments to them as she blessed them; and, as they put her to bed, said, "Oh God help me, my daughters, how tired I feel! it is more than twenty years since I went to bed so early."

The Duchess of Alba came frequently to visit her, much concerned for her old friend, whom she insisted on feeding with her own hand. She would sit down and embrace Teresa and draw the bed-clothes over her, but Teresa was worried lest an unpleasant smell from a bottle of oils that had accidentally been upset over the bed should annoy the duchess, whom she wished had not chosen to come at that time. The duchess, however, and the nuns also, assured her that far from detecting an evil smell, they believed the bed to have been sprinkled with water-of-angels,—the name of a scent then in use,—the duchess tactfully adding that she had been vexed to think scent should have been thrown on the clothes, as it might do the invalid harm. The invalid was, in point of fact, far beyond either remedies or harm. Violent haemorrhages of the lungs hastened her end. Not long after she had received the Sacraments, imploring God over and over again not to despise the offering of a humble and contrite heart, she sank into unconsciousness for fourteen hours, murmuring inaudible words, and died in the arms of Anna of St. Bartholomew on October 4th, 1582. She who had been born at dawn, died during the late evening.*

* The Gregorian reform of the calendar came into force the next day, making the alteration of ten days in our reckoning, and this is the reason why her feast is celebrated on October 15th.

They had asked her where she wished to be buried; did she wish her body to be taken to Avila? but she replied "Will they not give me a little earth here?" Accordingly, the coffin was placed in a hole cut in the masonry of the church at Alba, and heavily blocked in with bricks, stones, earth, lime and rubble, the nuns themselves assisting the workmen, for it seems that they already regarded her as a saint and were fearful lest the body should be stolen from them and removed to Avila. Her funeral had taken place in a strange mixture between the humility of the simple nun,—for officially she was nothing else,— and the honour voluntarily paid to one whom her contemporaries recognised as something far more. The Bishop of Salamanca and the Duke of Huescar had hurried to attend it, together with many monks and gentlemen of Salamanca and Alba. In conformity with custom, she had of course to be buried in her plain habit and veil,—and we know that her habit was patched and shabby, her veil often threadbare and worn inside out,—but they had done their best to counteract these signs of her chosen poverty by covering her bier with cloth of gold.

Supernatural graces had already preceded this temporal deference, during the hours between death and burial. Fragrance so strong had emanated from the body as the weeping nuns rendered it their last services, that they had been compelled to open the windows, not to be overcome. Miracles had also occurred, in the restoration of health and failing senses, as those pious women kissed the feet of their dead Foundress or pressed her hand against their brows. It was small wonder that they should regard the presence of her body in their church as their particular treasure and possession, to be protected from any marauder's hand.

But it so happened that the nuns of Alba were themselves the first to violate the grave. For nine months Teresa the traveller lay quietly at rest, entombed, her daughters coming frequently to pray beside the bricked-up scar in the wall; but little by little this solace ceased to suffice them and the desire grew upon them to look once more upon the lineaments that they had known. This desire, difficult and even grotesque as it may appear to our understanding, at length became irresistible. It was intensified, if not suggested, by the strange happenings they observed beside the grave: the scent of lilies, jasmine, and violets pervading the choir, and sometimes a scent to which they could give no name; moreover, should a nun drop off to sleep during her devotions, she would be recalled by sounds issuing from within the tomb. They awaited with growing impatience the arrival of their Father Provincial, now due to visit them, and immediately set about him, relating all that had taken place, and beseeching him to consent to a secret disinterment.

The scenes which followed should have been immortalised by El Greco, whose extraordinary vision alone could have done them justice. As a counterpart to the *Burial of the Count Orgaz* we should have gained, but far more fantastic and far more terrible, the *Exhumation of St. Teresa*. He was alive and active, painting at Toledo not so very far away; he should have been at Alba instead. He should have been making sketches from a corner of the dark church while others worked by candlelight. There in this masterpiece, for ever lost to us, lit by a violent chiaroscuro, would have moved the figures of the Father Provincial himself, with one other man, assisted by the nuns in their white habits and black veils, tremulously and industriously removing and setting aside the heavy stones on a heap of straw, and all the while in fear lest their proceeding should come to the ears of the redoubtable Duke of Alba. The elongated faces would have lost nothing of their expression of mingled guilt, agitation, and terror; the hands nothing of their carved muscularity as they tautened to grasp the stones; the robes nothing of their ample folds, falling forward and impeding the workers as they stooped. No opportunity here for his usual splendour of colour, for his greens, his sapphire-blues, his blood-red draperies, unless, indeed, he had opened the roof of the church to disclose, floating in Heaven, God the Father surrounded by a shoal of angels in a drift of rose-red banners and golden wings. But the illumination of amber and saffron should have sufficed him, turning the white cloaks to a yellowness of old ivory among the shadowed columns and the habits of the friars to bistre under the central brightness of the torches. What incident would the unseen sketcher have chosen? He had plenty of time to make a whole series of studies, for the labour took four days. Would he have been content to depict the two men shovelling rubble away while the women cleared? or would he have waited for the ghastly and hallowed moment when the broken lid of the coffin, finally lifted from the cavern, revealed the earth-stained features of the saint nine months dead?

The habit had rotted into damp and mouldy rags, but the body had preserved a miraculous incorruptibility. The nuns after performing the pious task of removing the clothes, scraping away the earth with knives, and washing the face and body, were able to look their fill and without repugnance before wrapping the mortal remains of Teresa in a clean sheet and restoring her for—as they mistakenly thought—the last time to her resting-place. But before that rite could be accomplished, there remained one act in this furtive drama, an act so grisly, so repulsive, that the imagination shudders at its contemplation. The Father Provincial advanced, and cut the left hand from the rigid arm. Veneration for saintly relics inspired him; and doubtless in the minds of the performer and the onlookers no shuddering recoil occurred, but only a pride of satisfaction that a tangible trophy should be carried from their great Foundress to the world. But for us the last touch of horror is added by the fact that that Father Provincial should be no other than the Father Gracian whom Teresa had so warmly loved, fretting lest he should injure himself by tumbling from his mule.

XVI

It might be thought that the reinterred Teresa would now be left in peace, but for those suspected of sainthood there is little repose. For two years the tomb was left undisturbed in the care of the nuns of Alba, who thought themselves secure in the possession of their treasure. They little knew that at the General Chapter of the Order, convoked at Pastrana, Father Gracian was advancing the claims of Avila to the body of its holy daughter. The indignation aroused by Teresa's first foundation at San José, when they had threatened to throw her into prison, was now quite forgotten, and even ironically reversed by the argument that San José had the right to her remains since she held the position of its Prioress at the time of her death. No one would have been more amused than Teresa at this working-out of human ways.

The Chapter had the grace to be concerned about the feelings of the nuns of Alba. It was realised that they would bitterly resent the deprivation, and it was therefore agreed that the removal of the coffin should take place in secret, the nuns being kept in ignorance until all was over, also that what remained of the left arm should be severed and left for indemnity in their keeping. This tactful plan went slightly wrong, for they had reckoned without Teresa. At the very moment the decision was come to in distant Pastrana three loud knocks, twice repeated, were heard within the tomb, startling the nuns who at first believed that someone had got shut into the church by mistake and dispatched the portress in all haste to release the prisoner. Their misgivings were allayed by the Prioress, who told them to pay no attention as it was evidently the Devil trying to disturb them.

The Prioress, with two of the older nuns, was taken into the secret when Father Gracian, Julian of Avila, three friars, and the Bishop of Palencia's secretary eventually arrived on their mission at the convent. Distressed though the women may have been, they could of course make no objection to the orders of their superiors. It was thought advisable however to get the flock of the community out of the way by sending them to sing Matins in the upper choir while the friars accompanied by the Prioress and the two nuns went to their task of reopening the tomb. The mysterious fragrance was again present; and the body, although rather more dried-up than before, was still uncorrupted within the cloths that had again rotted. This time it was observed that a cloak of white bunting, which had been used on her death-bed to staunch the flow of blood from her mouth and had been buried with her, was still bright red as though soaked in fresh blood and possessed the curious property of staining any piece of linen brought into contact with it. A further marvel was observed in the condition of the flesh, for when Father Gregorio de Nacianceno most reluctantly in "the greatest sacrifice ever imposed on him by obedience" inserted his knife under the truncated arm, the blade passed through with no more difficulty than if he were cutting a piece of cheese or a melon.

All had been carried out most clandestinely, according to intention, when the same suave and penetrating fragrance reached the upper choir and sent the nuns hurrying down in suspicion and alarm. They came too late; Father Gregorio was gone; and so, says the biographer, "they remained sadly with the arm of the Mother." Father Gregorio was on his way to Avila, and Teresa in her shroud with him, but not for ever.

Restless in her life, called a gad-about by a Papal Nuncio, Teresa had yet one more journey before her, the journey back from Avila to Alba. But before that could take place a flood of excitement swept over the Church and into Avila. The translation of the body had been known to few, for the wrath of the great ducal house of Alba was much dreaded, but the miracle of the incorruptibility was rumoured; it reached Madrid, it reached the ears of the King's confessor, it reached the Bishop of Cordoba, and finally travelled back to the Bishop of Avila who learnt of it from these two dignitaries in person. Despite the rigours of the season,—it was December,—they had journeyed from Madrid to investigate the matter for themselves. Teresa's small convent of San José received the Bishop, the confessor, two doctors, and a suite of twenty persons early in the morning on New Year's Day. Teresa was carried out into the gateway and placed upon a carpet. Nearly everyone present held a flaming torch; the Bishop knelt, bareheaded; most people were in tears. It is fortunately possible to reconstruct exactly what they saw:* "The body is erect, though bent a little forward, as with old people. It can be made to stand upright, if someone props it with a hand between the shoulders, and this is the position in which they hold it when it is to be dressed or undressed, as though it were alive. The colour of the body is of the colour of dates; the face darker, because the veil which was full of dust became stuck to it, and it was maltreated more than the rest; nevertheless it is intact, and even the nose is undamaged. The head has retained all its hair, as on the day of her death. The eyes having lost their vital moisture are dried-up, but the eye-lids are perfectly preserved. The moles on her face retain their little hairs. The mouth is tightly shut and cannot be opened. The flesh is that of a corpulent person, especially on the shoulders. (In the case of the severed arm, which he had held and hugged to his heart and closely examined, he had already noted that the flesh was wrinkled as in a once fat person who has grown thin.) The shoulder from which the arm has been detached exudes a moisture which clings to the touch and exhales the same scent as the body." The devoted friar was not in the least shocked by this close confrontation with the woman he had venerated. On the

---

* This description, in point of fact, was written by an eyewitness, Ribera, after a subsequent exposure of the body some twenty months later, but it is improbable that it had changed at all in appearance during the interval.

contrary, to his thinking it was the best day he ever had in his life, and he could not cease from admiring these holy remains.

Such, then, was the somewhat macabre spectacle offered to the Bishop of Avila and his suite at San José on that January morning—a withered and mummified image, the colour of dates, which could be propped upright by a hand placed between the shoulders. It lacked one arm, but the other hand was raised in the attitude of benediction. The devout and unimaginative Spaniards of course did not think it macabre at all; it was a panel that fitted only too naturally into the great composite reredos of sixteenth-century Spain; they gazed, they knelt, they wept, they adored, they felt increased and sanctified, proud and soul-stirred in their fanaticism that their land should have produced a major saint. The patron saint of Spain, as she stood there, rigid, and swaying slightly against the supporting hand.

The Bishop of Avila tried to keep the matter quiet, and even went to the length of threatening excommunication on any who should betray the secret, for it was feared lest the rapt of the body should come to the ears of the Duke of Alba. But so sensational an incident, witnessed by so many people, could not be hushed up. The news reached the convent at Alba, and tradition says that a lay sister surreptitiously slipped a note into a pie destined for presentation to the duchess. The duchess thereupon lost her head and her temper and ran frantically out into the street shrieking "They have taken Santa Teresa from me! they have taken the saint from me!"—a strange sight for the citizens of the little feudal town to behold. The imperious house of Alba was not likely to let such an insult pass. The duke himself was away in Navarre, where he was the hereditary Constable, but his uncle the Prior of San Juan who was in charge of his affairs sent off a messenger to Rome, demanding an order from the Pope for the instant return of Teresa's body.

It came. The order came, and Teresa followed it. Again she travelled in secret and by night, miraculously curing a monk of tertian ague on the way, and enticing some peasants who were threshing corn to drop their flails and follow the mysterious and seductive smell. No festivities were allowed to take place at Alba, by command of the Father Provincial who, much annoyed by the loss to Avila, had obeyed the Pope's order only because he could not well do otherwise. It was in the letter that he obeyed, not in the spirit. The body was merely

G

carried into the choir, and there was uncovered and illuminated, that the nuns might acknowledge it to be the true and recognisable remains of their Foundress. They were then required to hand over a formal receipt. But although all public rejoicings had been forbidden, nothing could prevent the rapturous crowd from pressing all day against the grille, and indeed it was fortunate that the iron bars were there to prevent them from tearing the clothes to pieces in their quest for relics; and not the clothes only, it was thought, but the body itself might have been in danger from those over-ardent fingers.

Ribera, Teresa's Jesuit biographer, knowing the temper of his countrymen, feared always that further outrages might be inflicted on the unfortunate corpse. Events proved him horribly right. As the legend of her sanctity grew, supported by innumerable miracles, the memory of the living Teresa faded and there remained in its place only the poor dried carnal husk which could be torn into morsels, endowed each one with miraculous properties. Even a fragment, however tiny, "even of the thickness of a finger-nail" preserved its incorruptibility as surely as a fleshless bone; and not its incorruptibility only, but that same strange penetrating scent. Ribera himself, who had noticed it clinging about his hands after his examination of the severed arm, and had hesitated to wash lest it should disappear, found that in spite of washing it persisted for about a fortnight. A novice who had been born with no sense of smell at all, acquired it suddenly and permanently after sniffing the hand which had been cut off by Father Gracian. This hand could do many things. It could destroy all other scents, however powerful; even the scent of musk smeared on to it with the tip of a knife. It could cure indigestion of twenty years' standing by merely being laid upon the stomach; it could cure the murderous jealousy of an injured husband by being laid upon the heart. Besides, many rags stained with her blood were by now widely distributed and proved no less efficacious; dying children were resuscitated, and the cracked skull of a citizen of Alba was repaired, by the application of pieces of linen which had touched her. What soul in superstitious Spain could fail to covet the possession of magical trophies such as these, or to take part in the scramble when opportunity offered? By the time Teresa was placed in her final resting-place above the High Altar in the much-rebuilt and glorified church at Alba, after the fifth opening of the coffin and public exposure of the body (in 1750), nothing but a horribly mutilated semblance remained of the once attractive girl or the humorous and alarming old reformer. It is painful to contemplate what had been done to her at various stages in the name of piety, but, shelving our cooler judgment and also the more gruesome fancies of a northern imagination, we must accept without argument that a passionate faith combined with a total lack of physical sensibility does lead men into very strange actions. A desire to possess some fragment of holy remains was of course so strong and so common as to over-ride all human queasiness or even a natural aversion to the idea of dismembering a once loved and revered person. An excessive example of ardour may be found in the case of the Portuguese lady who, on being allowed to kiss the foot of St. Francis Xavier, bit off a toe and carried it away in her mouth.

In Teresa's case this desire had led to what we should regard as a thorough desecration of the poor human shell. What had they done since Father Gracian started the process by cutting off one hand, and Father Gregorio de Nacianceno continued it by removing the rest of the arm? They had taken the right foot, and some fingers from the hand that was still raised in benediction; some ribs had been torn away from the side; pieces of flesh had been torn off for distribution among the crowd. Most ghastly of all, the head had been severed from the trunk, and most of the neck was missing, although they had honoured what was left of the neck by hanging around it a model of the collar of the Golden Fleece. The head itself, which now lay on a cushion of crimson satin enbroidered with silver, was in a pitiable condition. Part of the jaw had been taken, and the left eye was now an empty socket. But the other eye was intact even to its lashes and its pupil, as though it could still observe with glassy amusement the antics of the devout.

The heart, Teresa's warm heart, had been ripped out. When it was examined by surgeons and doctors in the eighteenth century and again in the nineteenth, some inexplicable things were found to have happened to it, though perhaps no more inexplicable than many other things which occur in the name of God. It had already been noticed, by peering through the openings of the reliquary in which the heart was kept, that mysterious thorns had sprouted from the dust at the base, about twenty in number, and it was believed that a new thorn appeared every time the Church passed through some special crisis. Unfortunately for the believers, a Commission appointed by the then Bishop of Salamanca investigated the miracle only to discover that the thorns were in reality bits of the feather brush which had been used to dust the reliquary. The Bishop, very sensibly, had them taken away. This was a disappointment, but there still remained the heart itself and the accompanying phenomena which could not be accounted for. It was wounded as though by a knife-thrust about an inch and a half in length, the edges of the wound being charred as though by some burning iron.* It seemed curious that those eyewitnesses who had described the exhumations should have made no mention of the gaping hole in the side which the extraction of the heart must have left, an omission which suggests that some unrecorded tampering took place later; but, whenever the robbery occurred and whatever pious interference may then have been practised in the desire to turn a unique relic into something even more striking than it already was, the faithful could find support and documentation in the fine and moving words of Teresa herself. It is the last vision we shall record of her, the vision of Crashaw's Flaming Heart, the vision which caused the Church to bestow upon her the title of "Seraphic," and which surely expunged from her memory all fearful recollection of the assaults of the Devil and of her descent into Hell. Satan she had seen, but now "I saw an angel close by me, on my left side, in bodily form. He was not large, but small of stature and most beautiful—his face burning, as if he were one of the highest angels, who seem to be all of fire. I saw in his hand a long spear of gold, and at the iron's point there seemed to be a little fire. He appeared to me to be thrusting it at times into my heart and to pierce my very entrails; when he drew it out, he seemed to draw them out also, and to leave me all on fire with a great love of God. The pain was so great that it made me moan; and yet so surpassing was the sweetness of this excessive pain that I could not wish to be rid of it. The soul is satisfied now with nothing less than God. . . ."

The physical aspect of miracles may be negligible; unexplained, though capable of some perhaps quite simple explanation, so far, on our long journey, hidden from us; the occasional frauds contemptible, practised with the best intentions by the over-eager, over-reaching, avid, fanatical devout. The true miracle is that such intimations should exist in the soul, satisfied with nothing less than God.

* See appendix, p. 177.

St. Thérèse of Lisieux

1873–1897

❧

I

IN the month of September 1843 a young Frenchman aged twenty presented himself at the monastery of the Grand St. Bernard and demanded admittance, not as an over-night guest but as a prospective inhabitant for life.

The Prior, to whom this request was brought, decided personally to interview the traveller. His claims and credentials were pitiably few for an aspirant to the monastic calling in the Cistercian Order. He was compelled to confess that he had not yet even completed his studies in Latin, whereupon the Prior, kindly and regretful, sent him on his way. "Do not be disheartened," he added; "go back to your own country, work hard, and then we will receive you with open arms."

The young man did go back to his own country but never returned to claim the promised welcome on the Alpine pass. A different fate awaited him: he was destined to marry, to be struck by paralysis, and to lose his reason, but not before he had become the father of the most gently remarkable of Saints. Thérèse of Lisieux owed her existence to the fact that Louis-Joseph-Stanislas Martin failed to get himself accepted as a postulant and returned to Alençon in Normandy to marry Marie-Zélie Guérin instead.

Mlle. Guérin was a profoundly religiously minded young woman exactly suited to the man she was to espouse, and moreover had already suffered a disappointment similar to his own. It had been her desire to enter the Order of St. Vincent de Paul, but on presenting herself for an interview the Mother Superior had replied quite simply and without hesitation that such was not God's will. It looked almost as though God Himself had intervened to inspire both the Prior and the Prioress in their refusals. . . . A further intervention of Providence was likewise noticed: the families of the two young people were not on terms of acquaintance, although their social standing was much the same and Alençon only a small provincial town; they did not live in the same parish and were in fact unaware of each other's existence. It was necessary for the purposes of Providence that they should in some way be brought together, and it appears that the first meeting took place on the Dantesque model half-way across the Pont St. Leonard, over the river Sarthe, when he stood civilly aside to let her pass. We know nothing of the further stages which finally brought them to the altar in Notre Dame d'Alençon in July 1858. He was then thirty-five and she was twenty-eight.

Ever since her rejection by the Mother Superior of the convent of St. Vincent de Paul, Zélie had deliberately turned her thoughts in another direction. God had not chosen that she should serve Him in the way her inclinations suggested, but, since she was determined to devote herself to Him at all costs, she now made it her constant prayer that He might send her many children, all of them to be dedicated to His service. It must therefore have come as somewhat of a disappointment to her when her bridegroom, on their wedding night (and apparently not until then) announced his intention of regarding her always as his sister rather than as his wife. Still, in her submissiveness, she fell in with his wishes, and for many months they lived together under these conditions, M. Martin occupied with his business as a watch-maker and jeweller, Mme. Martin with her own business as a lace-maker. It was a peaceful and devout existence. On Sundays their shop remained closed despite the protests of their friends. Why, they were asked, could they not at least leave a side-door open to admit the holiday-making young peasants coming into the town from the neighbouring villages? The shutters would be down, it would look outwardly as though the shop were closed, yet their sales would be assured. M. Martin was not ashamed to reply that he preferred the blessings of God. Upright and industrious, he allowed himself only one recreation, when he occasionally joined that patient string of anglers without which no French river-bank is complete. Even so, the eels and trout which he drew from the Sarthe were not put to his personal benefit but were instantly conveyed to the necessitous convent of the Poor Clares.

Every morning at an early hour the couple were to be seen kneeling together before the altar; the fasts and abstinences of the Church were faithfully observed in the house; while for their favourite relaxation they had recourse to pious books. It was not only their duty, but their inclination, to render tribute to the God whose Hand was apparent in every circumstance of their lives; He it was who had enabled them to recognise one another when, total strangers, they passed in the street; He it was, or perhaps our Lady speaking for Him, who had impelled Mme. Martin to take up her profession with the command "Make Point d'Alençon !"She remembered the exact date and occasion: it was on the 8th of December, the Feast of the Immaculate Conception, when she was busy with other things and for once not thinking of the dowry she must accumulate if she wished to marry and become the mother of servants of God. Heaven had certainly ordered their ways; the only thing lacking was those very servants of God she had so ardently desired.

Gradually, however, by steps which no information enables us to follow, the personal situation modified itself between Mme. Martin and her husband, and as one writer delicately puts it, "nine white flowers germinated in this chosen flowerbed." Four little girls came first, Marie-Louise, Marie-Pauline, Marie-Léonie, and Marie-Hélène, but in spite of many tears and petitions the absorbing desire of the parents for "a little priest" or "a little missionary" remained unsatisfied. Finally, thanks, they believed, to the intercession of St. Joseph whose aid they had invoked, a boy, Marie-Joseph, was born, but departed from this life at the age of five months. His younger brother, another Marie-Joseph, survived for nine months, but after this second loss the prayers for a little missionary ceased: the parents had decided that it was evidently not God's will. "For my thoughts are not your thoughts, neither are your ways my ways, saith the Lord."

Mme. Martin had need of all the resignation at her command. She had to suffer not only the deaths of her two little sons, but also of Marie-Hélène who died of consumption at the age of four, and of Marie-Mélanie who came in a second batch of sisters and died at three months. But her faith and her living belief in another world sustained her. "As I closed my children's eyes," she wrote, "I heard people saying that they had better never been born. I could not endure this way of talking, as I could not admit that our griefs and cares deserved to be weighed against the eternal happiness of my children. Besides, they are not lost for ever. Life is short and full of misery; I shall find them again on high."

Although she had buried four children, Mme. Martin was still left with another four. It was at about this time (1871) that M. Martin's earthly prosperity allowed him to retire from trade and to transfer himself and his family into a more convenient house on the steep rue Saint-Blaise, recently inherited from Mme. Martin's father. M. Martin had given up his watch-making and jewellery, but Mme. Martin continued to carry on with her Point d'Alençon. She preferred to do so, quite apart from the fact that she sometimes received as much as 500 francs (£20) a yard for it. She was happiest, she said, sitting at her window fitting together the strips and pieces of lace prepared by her work-girls under her supervision; and indeed one may readily believe that there is something very soothing about the mechanical occupation of the lace-maker with her pillow and her bobbins, something analogous to the telling of the rosary, something peculiarly suited to the life of intense and inward meditation. Point d'Alençon, as it happens, is made entirely by the needle, but still it should have seemed significant to observe how small threads gradually made complete patterns. Unfortunately we have no means of knowing whether this pertinent simile ever occurred to Mme. Martin's imagination.

She was due, however, soon to experience something startlingly removed from the peaceable routine of the rue Saint-Blaise. She was sitting alone one evening, quietly reading in the Lives of the Saints, when she suddenly felt her shoulder clutched by something which she afterwards described as the claws of a wild animal (une griffe de bête féroce). Knowing herself to be for the ninth time pregnant, she was at first considerably alarmed, and although she speedily recovered her trust in God it was not until some time later that she was able to connect this strange occurrence with the anger of the Powers of Darkness against the unborn child.

II

THE baby, born towards midnight on January the 2nd, 1873, and christened Marie-Françoise-Thérèse two days later, was so delicate that her mother almost despaired of her life. It must be admitted that the mother was herself partly to blame, owing to her disregard of the doctor's advice and her reluctance to put the baby out to nurse; but now, forlorn in M. Martin's absence, she realised bitterly that she was incapable of nursing her own child and hung over it for the whole of an agonised night alone, waiting for the dawn. Day was breaking as she left Alençon on foot for the village of Sémallé, two leagues away, in search of Rose Taillé, a peasant's friendly wife, already known to her. Weary and exhausted, for her confinement lay not so very far behind her, she arrived at the cottage just as the peasant household was stirring to the day's work. Her arrival created some consternation, for in the eyes of the humble Taillés Mme. Martin was *une dame* who should not tramp the country lanes unaccompanied at such an hour. The poor lady, they argued, must indeed have found herself in a plight to take so drastic and unconventional a step. Together the two women set hastily out on the return to Alençon along the wintry roads.

Thérèse was apparently dying when they reached the rue Saint-Blaise; the life which has now influenced millions was on the point of fading away. So slender was the hope, that at one moment the mother rushed in despair to her own room to pray for the passing of yet another infant soul. But Rose Taillé, the humble instrument, carried the fount of physical life within her, and the two women watched as the baby drank feebly at that warm natural source.

It was necessary to take Thérèse out to Sémallé, for Rose could not abandon her own children, and there, after some vicissitudes (within three weeks Thérèse was again given up for lost, this time with intestinal trouble) her perilous beginnings changed gradually to the normal health of a country-bred child. The cottage was simple: three-roomed and thatched, close to the usual farm-buildings, byres, and middens, a real Normandy homestead, where for fifteen months Thérèse was trundled about in a wheelbarrow full of hay, or was carried in Rose's apron when Rose went out to milk the cow. The cow was large and friendly; she was called La Rousse, and would allow the baby to be held on her back for a ride. There were other days when Thérèse was taken into Alençon with Rose to sell the butter and be shown to her parents—a regular and placid existence with the orchards and buttercups for its background. Thérèse was plump and gay and extremely self-willed when she returned to Alençon to become the pet of her family household.

There may be no significance in the fact that her father was already fifty when she was born, but it seems that he idolised this child as he had never idolised any of the others. Admittedly, the milieu is the small French bourgeoisie in a small provincial town at a date when the domestic virtues and affections were particularly highly esteemed,— and even to-day the French family tie is notoriously close, and French children notoriously spoilt according to English ideas,—but even so M. Martin's familiar endearments strike us as slightly extravagant. Thérèse was known as his "little queen," and when in a particularly jocose mood he would add "of France and of Navarre." Perhaps it is somewhat unfair that these intimate exuberances should ever have been exposed outside the circle of his family—even the wisest amongst us are apt to speak foolishly to our children or our dogs in private— but they may be taken as indicative of the playful, tender atmosphere prevailing in the rue Saint-Blaise, nor is it irrelevant to suggest that both the manner and the attitude had a considerable influence on Thérèse's later development. How could it be otherwise? The favourite adjectives in her parents' vocabulary were "dear" and "little"; sweet-ness was the rule of the house. Many letters from Mme. Martin have been preserved in which she relates with loving detail the smallest actions and sayings of her children, more especially of Thérèse whom she regarded as precocious in charm and angelic virtue. The family life emerges with complete intimacy: Thérèse creeping into her sister's bed and calling out to the servant, "Let me alone, poor Louise, you must see that we are like two little white chickens, you can't separate us"; Thérèse clambering up the staircase, stopping on every step to call out "Maman! Maman!" She was loving, demonstrative, and, even at the age of three, pathetically anxious to be good ("*Maman, je vais être bien mignonne*"), but at the same time so lively and inquisitive that she got called by other names, "little imp," "little ferret," as her mother wondered how she would turn out. "So tiny, such a mad-cap, a very intelligent child, but much less docile than her sister, and, above all, of an almost invincible obstinacy. When she says No, nothing will make her yield. You could put her into the cellar for a whole day without getting a Yes from her; she would sooner sleep there." She was proud, too. "My little Thérèse, if you will kiss the ground I will give you a sou." "Oh no, my little mother, I would rather go without the sou." Yet evidently she had the grace of contrition already within her, for one night after her mother had manifested displeasure and had left her in her bed, she heard the sound of sobs and there was Thérèse beside her, barefoot, stumbling over her long nightgown, begging for forgiveness.

This fond family, however, was soon to be disrupted, for when Thérèse was only four-and-half poor Mme. Martin at the age of forty-six succumbed to a disease from which she had long been suffering, cancer of the breast. A pilgrimage to Lourdes had been undertaken, but although she had entered the piscina four times, sitting in icy water up to her shoulders, no improvement had resulted. She came back to Alençon to die. The two youngest children, Céline and Thérèse, were kept out of sight of their mother's sufferings, which had now become severe, but when the dire moment arrived for Extreme Unction to be administered the little girls were brought into the room to witness the ceremony. Thérèse remembered all her life the exact corner of the room where she had been told to kneel; she remembered being taken back next day and lifted up by her father to kiss the death-cold forehead; she remembered suddenly finding herself alone in the corridor, confronted by the coffin propped upright; she had never seen one before but she knew instantly what it was, and, so small was she, only by raising her head could she contemplate it in its entirety.

III

M. MARTIN, whose hair and beard had gone white, was now left with the care of his five surviving daughters, and decided to transport them to Lisieux where he could depend on the help of his wife's brother and sister-in-law, M. Guérin, a chemist, and Mme. Guérin.

A house was found for them, and found quickly: Les Buissonnets, which one might translate as The Shrubbery, on the outskirts of the small and hilly town. It lay up the slope of a winding path just off the road which leads to Trouville, in a real shrubbery of a secluded garden, thickly planted in parts with laurel, thuya, euonymous, and ivy. The architecture of the house was of a glaring red with ornamentation of lacy rustic woodwork painted white, crowned by a belvedere in the roof which commanded views over the roofs of Lisieux and the pleasant surrounding country. M. Martin took this belvedere as his study for his hours of retirement; it was an understood thing that he should not be interrupted there, but his favoured Thérèse, *sa Benjamine, sa petite reine*, might always clamber the stair with the certainty of her welcome:

> J'aimais encore, au belvédère,
> Inondé de vive lumière,
> À recevoir les doux baisers d'un père,
> À caresser ses blancs cheveux
> Neigeux.

Thus the belvedere, although aesthetically speaking it added nothing to the architectural attractions of the house, did supply something with its seclusion and its wide windows to the solitary man and the affectionate child. For the rest, Les Buissonnets was precisely the sort of house we see standing "in its own grounds" at the approach to any of our own large towns and according to our standards of taste was both ugly and, for its size, pretentious. Anything less like the gaunt forbidding palace at Avila could scarcely be imagined than this *chalet bourgeois*. The furniture put into Les Buissonnets by M. Martin matched it inevitably. Heavy and highly polished mahogany; a circular table on one central leg; a side table in the dining-room with carved rabbits, pheasants, and partridges; a clock under a glass case on the mantlepiece; engravings after David on the walls. It is still there to-day, strangely eloquent, and touching even in its hideousness; certain alterations have been made inside the house and the furniture pushed unnaturally against the walls, giving it the air of a museum which indeed it is; but the garden remains very much the same as it was, with its heavy greenery, its stray and spiky yuccas, its oval flower-bed set in the middle of the front lawn, its wash-house where, in a neglected corner,

Thérèse had her own garden. She planted periwinkles in it and ferns; she decorated it with shells and pebbles and bits of wood; she made an altar and put flowers on it; one expects to see her come running round the corner, but her toys, instead of being left about all over the grass, are indoors as precious relics now: her skipping-rope, her miniature oven, her toy piano, the cage for her canary, her draught-board, her sailing-boat, her doll in the bassinette, all preserved even as her long golden curls hang in a glass case in the church down in the town. Her very modernity, her closeness to us in date, make the material legacy of St. Thérèse so multiple, so personal, so detailed. Whatever doubts may be cast upon the relics of other saints, these at least are incontrovertible.

Thérèse had not minded leaving Alençon. As she herself wrote later on in this connexion, children enjoy change and anything unusual. She thought Les Buissonnets charming (*cette riante habitation*), and so it must have appeared to a child who had always lived cramped in a house giving on to a street; and as she grew older there were many treats she could enjoy: she was old enough now to go fishing some-times with her father in the river Touques, taking a little rod of her own, and every afternoon she went for a walk with him, which led them sometimes into a church to visit the Blessed Sacrament, and sometimes into the chapel of Carmel. "Look, my little queen, behind that big grating are holy nuns who constantly pray to God." At this time also she began to go to confession; well instructed by her sister, she knew exactly what she had to do, but alas, when she knelt the top of her head did not reach to the ledge, and the priest, peering through his grille in search of his penitent, failed to perceive her. The greatest of modern saints was at that moment also the smallest: she was too small to be seen. Back at Les Buissonnets again, she had her lessons to do, and remembered always that the word "heaven" was the first word she ever learnt to read; then she must arrange her own indoor altar, which she was allowed to do for herself before saying her prayers. She had her own flower vases for it, but everything was on so small a scale that a couple of tapers could do duty for candles in the tiny candlesticks. Sometimes Victoire, the servant, would give her two ends of real candles as a surprise; but this was very seldom. During the winter evenings, after a game of draughts, Marie or Pauline read the Liturgical Year, and then some pages out of an improving book,

when Thérèse climbed onto her father's knees, leant her head against
his heart, and listened half asleep while he sang to her and rocked her
in his arms. The description is her own, for she remembered every
detail of their simple familiar life and did not hesitate to set it down;
in her heedless fluency she was a born autobiographer. Even to the
games she played with her cousin Marie, relating how they amused
themselves by walking along the street hand-in-hand with their eyes
shut, pretending to be blind, until they fell over a pile of empty boxes
standing on the pavement, and by the clatter brought the shopkeeper
out in a rage.

How different was the mild life and amusement of these little girls
from that of the Spanish children running away to Africa to get
themselves beheaded by the Moors, or trying to build caves for
anchorites within the walls of their father's palace! How different
their reading—the Liturgical Year at Les Buissonnets, the preposterous
romances of mediaeval chivalry at Avila!

It seems, however, from her own telling, that the young life of
Thérèse Martin was not altogether so mild and normal as it might
appear on the surface, for her mother's death had affected her profoundly. She had not cried much, nor had she told anyone of the
sorrow in her heart. But, "you know," she writes, addressing herself
to her sister, "that my happy nature changed completely after maman's
death. I, so lively, so expansive, became timid and gentle, and exag-
geratedly sensitive; a book often sufficed for me to dissolve into tears;
nobody must take any notice of me; I could not endure the company
of strangers. . . . Ah, if God had not lavished His beneficent rays on
His little flower, she would never have been able to acclimatise herself
on this earth." It is hard to believe that a child of four could be so
affected, but Thérèse was no ordinary child in spite of her gaiety, her
mischief, her stubbornness, and her pretty ways, and her unusual
quality was beginning to reveal itself.

We do not know what M. Martin made of it all, when, for example,
Thérèse informed him that her name was written in heaven. She had
discovered, as she thought, a T in the constellation of Orion, very
comprehensibly, for it stands out plain on a bright winter night. We
do not know either what he thought when she prevailed upon her
sister Pauline to present her to the Mother Prioress at the Carmel,
and besought her to accept her as a postulant. The Prioress listened,

only to reply gravely that one could not accept postulants of nine years old, and that Thérèse must wait until she was sixteen. Perhaps M. Martin, hearing this story, remembered his own thwarted attempt on the Grand St. Bernard. Least of all do we know what he thought of an extraordinary occurrence which took place at about this time and which seemed to indicate that his Thérèse, unlike himself, might really be intended for the devotional life. It was shortly after his second daughter, Pauline, had herself taken the veil at Carmel. The loss of her sister came as such a bewildering blow to Thérèse that she was seized with strange and violent tremblings all over her body and finally fell so ill that her life was in danger. Prayers and masses, as was natural to that pious household, were offered up for the recovery of the beloved child, but neither prayers, tears, nor medical aid seemed to produce the slightest amelioration. Thérèse lay small and moaning in her bed; terrifying visions assailed her, accompanied by shrieks of fear; some nails driven into the walls of her room appeared to her as the stumps of charred fingers; her sisters dared not leave her alone for a moment. A day came when, crying out for Marie, Thérèse failed to recognise her. Her sisters in alarm threw themselves with supplications before a statue of our Lady; three times did they repeat their prayer and at the third repetition they saw Thérèse fix her eyes on the image for four or five minutes "with a radiant look as though she were in ecstasy," when she turned towards Marie with a renewed and tender recognition. From that moment onwards all sign of her illness disappeared, and by the next day she was able to resume her normal life.

Thérèse later wrote her own version of what had happened during those miraculous minutes. "Finding no help on earth and on the point of dying of sorrow, I turned towards my Mother in Heaven, praying with all my heart that she might take pity on me. Suddenly, the statue came to life. The Virgin Mary became beautiful, so beautiful that I shall never find words to render that divine beauty. . . . The Holy Virgin advanced towards me. She smiled to me—ah, how happy I am! I thought, but I shall tell no one or my happiness will vanish."*

This reluctance to confide details of her vision—a reluctance which

---

* It may be of interest to remark that the statue in question was a reproduction of a silver statue by Bouchardon, originally in the church of St. Sulpice, in Paris. The original disappeared during the Revolution.

is perhaps the most convincing proof of genuine credence, shared by
Thérèse with many other saints—was overcome by Marie who, as a
witness of the occurrence, had already formed some idea of what had
taken place. "When I found myself alone with her," writes Thérèse,
"I could not resist her tender and pressing questions. In surprise at
finding my secret discovered without my having spoken a single word,
I confided it entirely to her. Alas, I had not been mistaken, my happiness was to vanish and be changed to bitterness. . . ."

Marie rushed to Carmel with the great news of an authentic miracle,
and Thérèse was summoned to give her own account. Received by
the Mother Superior in person, she was immediately surrounded by
nuns who besieged her with questions. There were many things they
wanted to know. Had the Holy Virgin been carrying the Child Jesus?
had she been escorted by angels? Thérèse was deeply troubled by
their insistence, and would reply only under pressure that the Holy
Virgin had looked very beautiful and had advanced towards her with
a smile. Then, observing that the nuns had expected something quite
different, and were in fact disappointed, she began to imagine that
she herself had invented the whole story. It is a pathetically true touch
of a child's nature. Another child, far from evading the flattery im-
plicit in the cross-examination, might have exaggerated and embroidered as she observed the avid attention of her listeners. The child
is a born play-actor after all, when once it has departed from its natural
secretiveness, and takes its cue from its audience. Not so Thérèse.
Many years went by before she recovered from what she regarded as
this betrayal and humiliation; years during which she suffered a darkness
of remorse to be understood only by those who have also endured
the torment of a super-sensitive and scrupulous conscience. "Ah!" she
exclaimed, "if only I had kept my secret to myself I should also have
kept my joy." This extreme delicacy of feeling, this excitability both
in sorrow and in enjoyment, characterised her from her earliest age,
and persisted throughout her life; she was a mixture between the
firmly and the finely poised, never deviating from the main line of
her intention yet trembling with sensibility all along the way. Expansive by nature, she retained the fundamental reserve proper to
those who live with strings too acutely tautened. "There are some
things," she wrote, "which lose their scent when exposed to the air;
there are intimate thoughts which cannot be translated into the language

of this earth, without instantly losing their profound and heavenly meaning." The phrase is applicable also to things other than celestial visions.

IV

FOR a person of her age—she was now ten—Thérèse had already lived through some considerable mental experiences. She had lost her mother; she had lost her sister, though in a different way; she had taken her own resolution to embrace the cloistered life, not on any impulse but knowing fully what it meant; she had suffered the disillusion of having her entreaty rejected; she had lain at death's door; she had seen our Lady appear to her; she had become the centre of a most unwelcome interest in the convent parlour; she had thereafter plunged into a deep and durable grief, a grief which now added itself to the sum of her piling knowledge. Life itself supplied the arduous novitiate she had desired. She was not built to take experiences lightly and, already matured beyond her years, in spite of the skipping-rope, the little oven, and the sailing boat, she now prepared to face another set of events which, in their different ways, proved no less agitating than the others. She had already been sent to school at the Benedictine convent, where, although she returned to Les Buissonnets every night, she was not too happy. She was bad at games, incongruous as it may seem to associate the importance of games with a convent school for girls at Lisieux in 1881; she shrank from her companions, who were too rampageous for her taste, and who in their turn teased her. Neither her application to her lessons nor her successes in class increased her popularity. But all this was as nothing compared with the emotion aroused in her by her first communion. It was a moment to which all else had been a preparation, and with the rapture of first love she received it. "Ah, how sweet was the first kiss of Jesus to my soul! Yes, it was a kiss of love! I felt that I was loved, and I said also, 'I love you, I give myself to you for ever.' Jesus asked nothing of me, He required no sacrifice. He and the little Thérèse had long since looked at one another and had understood. That day, our meeting could no longer be called a simple look, but a *fusion*. We were no longer two."

H

This revealing passage, with sentiments reproduced a hundred times throughout the pages of Thérèse's autobiography, conveys very exactly and convincingly the absolute abandonment of self into the keeping of another; the absolute submergence in union; the entire surrender, the fusion as Thérèse with her final cry in her search for the right word, calls and italicises it. She may or may not have known that it was the recognised word appropriate to the experience. The language is the language of human love; it is amorous; it is passionate; it is the bride finding herself for the first time in the arms of her lover. The soul knows no other means of expression in words; and although the phraseology so familiar in the relation of human passion may jar and even offend where applied to so transcending a revelation, those who have known both the first ecstasy and the subsequent meticulous loyalties of human devotion will more rightly estimate the exactitude of the metaphor. Thérèse was henceforth truly and mystically wedded to Jesus.*

The need, the desire to consecrate her outward life to the summons she had inwardly answered, naturally grew even stronger. Like genius, it was irresistible; it consumed her, a fire which could not be smothered. The entry of her sister Marie into Carmel was yet another blow to be borne, but her loss had only the effect of making Thérèse turn more and more towards Heaven. It is indeed pitiful to read the struggles of her young soul, torn between the vision of perfection, the galling delay, and the despair of the "dark night" which sometimes assailed her. Of her own disposition at that time she writes with her usual candour that her excessive sensibility rendered her truly unbearable. No doubt she exaggerates, and no doubt the chief sufferer from her temperament was Thérèse herself, so prone to tears and then so ashamed of having shed them that she would start to weep again for having wept. Her heroine Jeanne d'Arc had also been much inclined to tears but her predecessor Teresa of Avila had had no patience with them.

---

* For the benefit of Catholic readers, who may be puzzled at the belated date of Thérèse's first communion, it should be explained that in the diocese of Bayeux, to which Lisieux belonged, it was ordained that every first communicant should have attained the age of eleven during his year of admission, but as Thérèse's birthday fell on January 2nd she missed the privilege by two days. She herself was much distressed at this hindrance, and her sister Marie had some difficulty in stopping her from running after the Bishop of Bayeux when she caught sight of him in the street.

The cause, Teresa said in her sensible way, might be an accumulation of humour round the heart, which had a great deal more to do with it than the love of God.

Then occurred an incident which Thérèse refers to as her "complete conversion," as though conversion were the term to use for one whose eyes from childhood had turned always in the same direction. It happened on Christmas day, at one o'clock in the morning. Thérèse, then aged nearly fourteen, on returning to Les Buissonnets after attending the midnight Mass, knew well that in the chimney-corner would be standing the French child's equivalent of our Christmas stocking—her own shoes filled with treats and presents. Hitherto, her father had always genially watched her pleasure and had listened with increasing cheerfulness to her cries of delight as she drew first one thing and then the other from the enchanted shoes; but on this occasion, for some reason, he seemed glum and bored, and as Thérèse mounted the staircase she heard him remark, "This is really too babyish a surprise for a big girl like Thérèse; I hope this will be the last year of it."

The effect of these words upon Thérèse was startling; they pierced, she says, her heart. Céline who had followed her whispered, knowing her well, "Don't go downstairs again yet, wait a little; you will cry too much as you look at the surprises in front of Papa." The brief scene seems small though touching—the two little girls whispering together on the landing, the bearded father standing below, unconscious of what he had done, the shoes waiting on the hearth by the fire—but such things are not small even to a normal child. Thérèse had been stabbed. She behaved however very differently from Céline's expectation. Running downstairs, she made straight for her shoes and joyfully pulled out everything; Papa was no longer bored; he was laughing now; he had no idea of this victory over self which had moulded Thérèse for ever in the space of five minutes. She had "recovered for always her strength of soul, which she had lost at the age of four-and-a-half."

Thérèse describes this Christmas night as the opening of the third and happiest period of her life. It is curious that she should see her life so clearly divided, especially when we consider what immature years she is dealing with, but evidently in her mind there stood up, like mountain passes dividing one valley from another, the three events of her mother's death, her first communion, and her "complete conversion." To us, seeing it in perspective, her life appears as a straight line, drawn from point A to point Z with no deviation, no arabesques of pattern. But the soul knows its own history best. Thérèse saw, and saw instantly, that her childhood had ended; that her tremors must end also; that the way which was her own discovery lay clearly before her; she had but to follow it in the minutest scruple; it was the way which would lead her to sainthood. As though looking once over her shoulder into the past, she wrote a retrospective farewell. Thérèse was not a great poet, although she frequently expressed herself in verse; the debt to Chateaubriand here is obvious, but the stanzas have the charm of autobiographical simplicity:

    * Oh! que j'aime la souvenance
      Des jours bénis de mon enfance!
      Pour garder la fleur de mon innocence
        Le Seigneur m'entoura toujours
          D'amour.

      J'aimais les champs de blé, la plaine;
      J'aimais la colline lointaine;
      Dans mon bonheur je respirais à peine,
        En moissonnant avec mes sœurs
          Les fleurs.

      J'aimais la paquerette blanche,
      Les promenades du dimanche,
      L'oiseau léger gazouillant sur la branche.
        Et le bel azur radieux
          Des cieux.

      O souvenir, tu me reposes. . . .
      Tu me rappelles bien des choses . . .
      Les repas du soir, le parfum des roses,
        Les Buissonnets pleins de gaieté
          L'été.

    * A literal translation will be found on p. 181.

V

SOLE and singular inconsistency in a life so consistent in the spirit of humility throughout its short span, was her avowed conviction that she would one day achieve recognition as a saint. In secular life, a parallel self-confidence might incur a charge of arrogance: no youthful soldier admits even to himself that he will carry a Field-Marshal's baton in the fullness of his career. Even Teresa of Avila, who was arrogant enough in some matters, had adopted a more modest attitude, for when Fray Pedro de la Encarnacion told her that her presence had saved the city of Burgos from destruction by flood because she was a saint, she replied gravely, "Father, during my lifetime, I have been told that I was handsome and I believed it; that I was clever and I thought it was true; and that I was a Saint, but I always knew that people were mistaken on that score." Again, in her joking way, she had written that she used sometimes to be annoyed at hearing such foolish remarks as that she was a saint—if so it must be a half-and-half one, with neither feet nor head (*Ha de ser sin pies ni cabeza*). And again, she was delighted when someone said to her, "Well, Mother, you may be a saint, but you do not seem one to me." Yet Thérèse Martin, whose career was the epitome of especial abnegation, humility, and self-surrender, could openly aspire to the highest reward in the hierarchy of virtue. Although it is true that in the religious life the expression "to be a saint," "to become a saint" is used somewhat loosely according to mundane ideas, it seems evident from Thérèse's emphasis and also from many supporting phrases that she very definitely meant what she said. Doubts sometimes troubled her: "Truly, I am far from being a saint"; but even here the form of expression implies no renunciation of the ambition, only that she is still some way from its accomplishment. And the mood of dubiety, at best, is rare. Her more constant certainty breaks out in unequivocal phrases: "Reflecting then that I was born for glory, and searching for the means to attain it, it was inwardly revealed to me that my own glory would never appear to mortal eyes, but would consist in becoming a saint. This desire might seem full of temerity," she adds, "but I still feel the same audacious confidence that I shall become a *great saint*" (*une grande sainte*). The italics are hers. She had no essential doubts about her vocation, and one of the most interesting things about her is perhaps that in spite of her littleness she really made straight for the biggest, since, after all, to a religious person there could be no higher aim.

Her prophecies display the same temper. She had no doubt at all that her usefulness would not cease with her death but would be continued, and with far greater efficacy, from on high. God, she said, would do her will in Heaven because she had never done her own will on earth. She would give tangible proof of her celestial existence, she would send down showers of roses; she would do more, she would come down in person. Such assurances were frequent on her lips and in her writings. There was no mistrust of her own power, not because of any personal vainglory but because she was convinced that God was working through her.

The thought of any other profession which at moments crossed her mind, but which she instantly subjected to her determination to become a Carmelite and "the mother of souls," naturally ran along much the same self-sacrificing lines. To be a doctor, an apostle, a Crusader in defence of the Church, a missionary, a martyr—ah! what allurements she found in the contemplation of martyrdom! The dream of her youth, she calls it; but a single torture would not suffice her; she must undergo them all; she must be flagellated, crucified; like St. John she must be plunged into boiling oil; like St. Agnes and St. Cecilia she must offer her throat to the sword of the executioner; like St. Joan of Arc she must perish on the burning faggots, murmuring the name of Jesus. Such dreams remained hidden, fortunately for M. Martin and her sisters; no need to send the servant Victoire chasing up and down the streets of Lisieux, looking for a Thérèse who was running away to get herself beheaded by the heathen. But, although she had neither the temperament nor the tradition to put her romantic desires into practical execution, they were none the less active in her mind. Not content with looking back into the past, she sent her imagination forward also into the future, trembling at the thought that the incredible torments the faithful would suffer during the reign of the Anti-Christ could not all be reserved exclusively for her. Strange, smoky, bloody pictures to come out of the pleasant domesticity of Les Buissonnets! She knew however at the bottom of her heart that such aspirations were not for her; she must find another way of obtaining the crown of glory. But where to find that way?

St. Paul showed it to her as she read chapters xi and xii of the First
Epistle to the Corinthians:

Are all apostles? are all prophets? are all teachers? are all workers of miracles?
Have all the gifts of healing? do all speak with tongues? do all interpret? . . .

Though I give my body to be burned, and have not charity, it profiteth
me nothing.

Charity suffereth long and is kind; charity envieth not; charity vaunteth
not itself, is not puffed up.

Doth not behave itself unseemly, seeketh not her own, is not easily provoked,
thinketh no evil. . . .

Beareth all things, believeth all things, hopeth all things, endureth all
things.

Many had read these words before Thérèse, but few had grasped
as she grasped the possibilities of their extreme application.

"Seeketh not her own, is not easily provoked, beareth all things,
suffereth long. . . ." It was charity, then, charity and love, which
should provide the key to her search. "My vocation is love!" she exclaimed. "At last I have found it! I will be love itself! O luminous
lighthouse of love, I know how to reach you. . . . Love has chosen
me for its holocaust; me, weak and imperfect creature. . . . I have
no means of proving my love save by throwing flowers, that is to
say by neglecting no little sacrifice, no glance, no word, but to profit
by the slightest actions and to perform them for love. I want to suffer
through love and even to rejoice through love." Through the whole
of this ecstatic and even frenzied passage the key-word is the same; it
is the widening circle of the love she had yielded to Jesus the first
time she received Him and which was now to embrace every circumstance of life as she encountered it.

It does not seem to have occurred to her that she might practise
her philosophy in the ordinary world: her burning desire was con-
centrated solely on getting into Carmel there to abandon herself
utterly to her Beloved. There was no question of fear in her mind,
no devils threatening, only a devouring impatience to run, to run, to
be gathered to His heart. That was her goal, but many intolerable
obstacles stood in her way of reaching it. There was her age, and then
there was the necessity of obtaining her father's consent. From Céline
she had no opposition to fear, but she could not bring herself to

broach the subject to her father. His two elder daughters had already left him for the same reason; Céline was destined to take the veil before long; he was no longer young; he had already had one attack of paralysis which might at any moment be renewed; a poisonous insect had bitten him on the neck during one of his fishing expeditions, leaving him with a painful and apparently incurable growth. The poor white-haired widower was in no condition to receive such a request. Thérèse hesitated and hesitated. By Whitsuntide she had made up her mind to speak. M. Martin was sitting innocently in the garden, contemplating the beauties of nature; Thérèse, always sensitive to nature, describes the evening: the setting sun was touching the tops of the high trees and the birds were singing their evening prayers. Her eyes full of tears she went and sat beside him on the bench.*

They both wept; M. Martin began by saying that she was much too young to take so grave a decision, but finally, picking a flower he gave it to her saying that God had made it bloom and had preserved it until that day. Unlike Don Alonso de Cepeda, he had given his consent. This difficulty overcome, and her uncle's consent having also been obtained after a struggle, the next blow came in the shape of a message from the Superior of Carmel, M. le Chanoine Delatroëtte, to the effect that she could not be allowed to enter before the age of one-and-twenty. Thérèse had not expected this—it will be remembered that the Mother Superior had told her, when she was nine, that she must wait until she was sixteen, and it seems indeed that M. Delatroëtte was mistaken in his rigidity, for the rules of Carmel laid down no definite age limit for the novice as such, but insisted only that she should not make her solemn profession until she was seventeen. It was in vain that the Prioress endeavoured to persuade him. Her attempt produced an explosion of rage. "That girl again!" cried M. Delatroëtte. "One would really believe, to hear you, that the well-being of the community depended on the admission of that child. The establishment is in no danger. Let her stop with her father till she comes of age! Do you suppose, anyway, that I am refusing my consent without having consulted God? Let me hear no more of this affair!"

* Persons of any aesthetic susceptibilities, intending to visit Les Buissonnets, should take warning that the scene between Thérèse and her father has now been commemorated by a sculptural group executed in the purest white marble, and placed in the garden, representing them, slightly over life-size, sitting together on their bench.

Thérèse prevailed upon her father to take her into the presence of the obstructive cleric, who received her very coldly with a categorical *No*. But being a conscientious man he added that he was, after all, only the delegate of the Bishop of Bayeux, and that if Monseigneur chose to give his consent he would have nothing more to say. The Bishop was very kind indeed when Thérèse, accompanied by her father, penetrated into the episcopal palace. They were at first welcomed by the Vicar-General, M. l'abbé Révérony who, although he had himself arranged for the interview, seemed slightly surprised to see them. He too, however, was most friendly. Perceiving tears in Thérèse's eyes, he said, "Ah! I see diamonds. You mustn't show those to Monseigneur!" Thérèse was very much frightened by all the grandeur, and said that she felt like a tiny ant after being conducted through all those vast drawing-rooms, nor was her confusion diminished when M. Révérony made her sit in an enormous arm-chair, which could have accommodated four people of her size, in front of a brightly burning fire. She had hoped that her father might speak for her, but no, she had to plead her cause for herself and ended up by telling the Bishop that she had desired to give herself to God ever since she was three years old.

It is evident that the Bishop was surprised, touched, and rather amused, especially when M. Martin explained that in order to make herself appear older than she was she had put up her hair for the first time that morning. Thérèse was discomfited by this disclosure, and wished that Papa had not been so indiscreet, but the Bishop was sympathetic; he caressed her when in spite of M. Révérony's warning he saw tears in her eyes; he promised that he would speak to M. Delatroëtte, thereby causing Thérèse's heart to sink, for she knew well what the reply would be; he even escorted them down to his garden, told her that he was very glad to hear she was going on a pilgrimage to Rome with her father, and promised that she would have his answer on her return from Italy. She left, not having obtained much satisfaction, but another idea had already germinated in her mind.

VI

THRILLED though she naturally was by her journey—the splendours of Paris, the wild scenery of Switzerland, the cathedral of Milan, the cries of the gondoliers in Venice, the tongue of St. Anthony at Padua, the body of St. Catherine at Bologna—Thérèse kept her head and her judgment. "How interesting is the study of this world," she observed, aged fourteen, "when one is on the eve of quitting it." Nevertheless Rome was a tremendous excitement. All her desire for martyrdom flared up as she knelt to kiss the dust empurpled by the blood of the first Christians; and in the church of St. Agnes a minor miracle happened, which filled her with delight. She was beseeching the guide, in vain, to give her some relic of the saint for her sister Pauline who had taken the name St. Agnes of Jesus, when a little piece of red marble broke away from a mosaic and fell at her feet. "Wasn't that charming?" she writes. It was charming indeed, but the supreme moment was yet to come. Thérèse was even more alarmed than when she had sought out the Bishop of Bayeux, but at the same time she was absolutely resolved not to falter, for she knew that if she failed here there was no higher appeal on earth. The Prioress, M. Delatroëtte, the Bishop, and now the Pope. . . .

The scene amid the gilded splendours of the Vatican was impressive enough to the child from Les Buissonnets. Leo XIII, with his fine old eagle face, was seated in a raised chair, dressed in a white soutane and white tippit. Around him stood priests and ecclesiastical dignitaries. No one spoke; the pilgrims passed in single file, kneeling to kiss first the foot, then the hand of the Pontiff, and to receive his benediction. They were then silently moved on by two Papal Guards and their place taken by the next pilgrim.

Thérèse had formed the startling resolve to break this silence when her turn should come, a proof of no little courage considering the place, the occasion, and the reverential awe with which she of course regarded the Supreme Head of the Temporal Church. Fortunately, Papa had gone ahead and was already out of sight in the next room; but less fortunately M. l'abbé Révérony, the Vicar-General of Bayeux, was standing at the Pope's right hand; already acquainted with Thérèse, he had some inkling of this determined child's intention. As she approached the throne, he said suddenly and audibly that it was absolutely forbidden to speak to the Holy Father. Thérèse turned in distress to Céline who was just behind her.

"Speak!" Céline said.

The rest of the scene can be described in Thérèse's own words. "The next instant, I was at the Pope's knees. When I had kissed his slipper, he presented his hand to me. Then, raising towards him my eyes swimming in tears, I besought him in these terms, 'Most Holy Father, I have a great favour to ask of you.'

"Immediately, bending his head down to me, his face almost touched mine; it was as though his black and profound eyes wanted to penetrate me into the recesses of my soul.

" 'Most Holy Father,' I repeated, 'in honour of your Jubilee, allow me to enter Carmel at fifteen!'

"The Vicar-General of Bayeux, surprised and displeased, now intervened.

" 'Most Holy Father, this is a child who desires the life of Carmel, but the authorities are looking into the question already.'

" 'Well, then, my child,' said His Holiness to me, 'do whatever the authorities decide.'

"Clasping my hands then and pressing them down on his knees, I essayed one last effort.

" 'O! Most Holy Father, if only you would say yes, everyone would be willing.'

"He looked at me very fixedly and pronounced these words, weighting each syllable in a penetrating tone,

" 'Come now . . . come now . . . you will enter if God wills it.' "

Thérèse was about to speak again, when the Papal Guards required her to get up, but seeing that she would not move they each took her by the arm. The Vicar-General came to their assistance as she still remained with her hands clasped on the knees of the Pontiff. They took her away, but not before he had pressed his hand against her lips, blessed her, and watched her right out of sight. Thus the aged Pope and the little saint crossed once in their lives, met for an instant, and then were parted for ever.

VII

De la Suisse et de l'Italie,
Ciel bleu, fruits d'or, m'avaient ravie,
J'aimai surtout le regard plein de vie
Du saint vieillard, Pontife-Roi,
        Sur moi.

MEANWHILE the Bishop of Bayeux had been busy on Thérèse's behalf —though, disappointed at finding no word from him on her return to Normandy she did not omit to send him a note of reminder—and in April 1888 she finally entered Carmel. Her admittance comes almost as an anti-climax after all the turmoil and the struggle, and it is noteworthy that she herself, indefatigable recorder and analyst though she was, makes a relatively brief allusion to it. One would expect her to set down her finest shades of feeling, according to her custom, as she went through the ritual of initiation: the embrace given by every nun in turn, the few moments' solitude allowed her in her cell, the general prayer for her in the postulants' room, the donning of the black robe and veil, the shutting of the door against the familiar world. This ritual was not so awe-inspiring, certainly, as the ceremonies which would follow later, but the very fact of finding herself at last as an inhabitant within the sacred walls should have sufficed to rouse Thérèse to several pages of her lyrical outbursts. Not so. She seems to have taken it as a matter of course, as the inevitable. She records the human pang: "I threw a last glance towards Les Buissonnets. . . . I shed no tears, but, walking ahead to reach the cloister door, my heart was beating so violently that I wondered if I were going to die. Ah, what a moment! what an agony! It must be experienced to be believed." No more. For the rest, she had arrived in harbour and was embraced by the two sisters already anchored there.

M. Delatroëtte had considered it his duty to be present, but, for all the amiability he displayed, might have spared himself the trouble. He had been worsted, and he was not pleased. Making no attempt to accept his defeat with a good grace or to manifest the spirit of loving-kindness proper to his profession, he addressed the assembled nuns as follows: "Well! my Reverend Mothers, you can sing a Te Deum! As the delegate of Monseigneur the Bishop, I present to you this child of fifteen, whose entry you have desired. I trust that she will not disappoint your hopes, but I remind you that if it turns out otherwise, the responsibility will be yours alone." Thérèse herself was too charitable to record these remarks in her autobiography.

Her *prise d'habit* took place nine months later, when M. Martin, unexpectedly recovering in time from a second stroke, was able to be present, and Thérèse passed into the chapel on her father's arm. She was dressed, at his desire, in white velvet trimmed with swansdown and Point d'Alençon, a sheaf of white lilies in her hand and her long curls floating loosely over her shoulders. She was just sixteen. This second ceremony must be impressive and moving enough, yet again Thérèse makes no reference to it beyond dismissing it in the words "after the ceremony," without describing anything of her emotions or of what had taken place. We know what took place. The new novice is escorted into the convent by a procession chanting the Magnificat; she sees an avenue of white-habited nuns bearing lighted candles; the Cross is held out for her to kiss; kneeling before a grille, she listens to the voice of a priest emphasising the harsh life she must expect: the renunciation of all pleasures of the senses and even of the most innocent human pleasures, the hard work, the harder privations, the silence, the cold, the loneliness, from now onwards until death. She is then led away to have her hair cut short to her head, and is dressed in the brown tunic and the white veil, with the sandals on her feet; the black belt, symbol of servitude; the scapular, symbol of Christ's yoke; finally the great white cloak, symbol of candour and purity of heart. She will make no other change now, save that when she ceases to be a novice and takes her final vows, the white veil will be replaced by a black one and she will be given the long rosary and the big crucifix. Robed as a novice, she prostrates herself on the ground, her arms symbolically extended in the shape of the Cross.

Not M. Delatroëtte but the Bishop of Bayeux in person was present at the ceremony and again displayed a truly paternal benevolence towards Thérèse. He must have been a very charming man. In front of everybody he teased her, reminding her of her visit to the Palace and of how she had put up her hair for the first time that morning in order to appear older; then taking her shorn head between his hands, he gently caressed it. He could scarcely have foreseen then that thirty-four years later his successor in the Episcopal See would be celebrating the beatification of this child in St. Peter's, in the presence of forty-five archbishops and bishops, of all the ambassadors accredited to the Vatican, and an overflowing crowd of people.

It would seem, then, as though nothing remained to relate; as though the curtain came quietly down, leaving Thérèse in her bare cell, awaiting only the day when her profession should be complete. It was not likely that she would avail herself of the liberty which was still hers, to desert her calling and return to the world. No further events, in the worldly sense of the word, could happen to her now, except the greatest event of all which would begin in the convent infirmary and would end with her finding the entire perfection she sought. The rigours of the Carmelite life, so terrible to the lay mind in their severity, may here be indicated in order to give some idea of the daily detail of her existence, bearing in mind always that Thérèse had been accustomed to a comfortable home; to the blazing fires and soft beds of Les Buissonnets; to the homely comfort of the well-to-do bourgeois; the solid dining-room table with the good and plentiful food; the come-and-go and chatter of her sisters and cousins; the liberty of the garden; the presiding benevolence of her father, the friendly servant who gave one a candle-end as a special treat; the security which is the need of every child. In outward circumstances at least, Thérèse had always been suitably spoilt. Even when invited to kiss the ground for the bribe of a sou, she had not been compelled against her will to comply. All this was now exchanged for the austerity of Carmelite rule. There was now none of the frivolous laxity which had softened the days when Teresa had entered the Encarnacion; none of the gallant parties and conversations in the parlour; no peeping through doors, no receiving of titillating messages. Awakened at 5* by the dry clappering of castanets in the corridors,—a curiously Spanish sound which could not fail to evoke the image of the great reformer of Avila,—the recluse opened her eyes upon the denudation of her cell. She must not even think of it as "my cell," but as "our cell," since all private possession is forbidden. The walls are whitewashed; the window barred. The bed is a board placed across two trestles, with a paillasse and no linen, only woollen sheets, a woollen pillow, and a coarse blanket of felt. There is no chair, no

---

* The hour of rising was at 5 from Easter until September 14th, at 6 during the other months.

washstand, but since extreme cleanliness must be observed, a jug of water and a basin are placed on the floor. A writing-desk carries a work-basket and some devotional books. A crucifix, a holy water-stoup, and a religious picture hang on the walls, also a notice giving the constant reminder, "My daughter, what are you doing here?" A narrow wooden bench, and that is all. The cell measures nine foot by nine.

On rising, which she must do the moment she awakes, the recluse removes the scapular she has worn during the night, also the veil which has covered her head, replacing them by the tunic and the habit; and, on her head, the *toque* ordained by Teresa of Avila. Of plain linen, it enwraps the head and throat, while leaving the forehead bare, because its designer with her respect for the things of the intellect did not approve of a bandaged brow. Over the *toque* goes a veil, and not more than five pins must be used to secure it. On the feet go the *alpargates*, most Spanish of all these Spanish echoes, for they are the traditional sandal of the Spanish peasant, fastened with a strap of plaited hemp. Thus sixteenth-century Spain, with the rattle of the castanets and the shuffle of the sandal, wakes again in nineteenth-century Lisieux, and the magnificent Castilian Teresa lays as it were a direct touch daily at dawn on the little French Thérèse.

Rules in the convent are strict. Silence must be observed as far as possible, whether at work or at meals. At work you break the silence only when it is not practicable to communicate by signs. At meals, which are preceded by a bell summoning you to an examination of your conscience and by a two-by-two procession into the refectory intoning the De Profundis, you sit under the grim reminder of a skull hanging on the wall, and may speak only in order to make public confession of some fault. If this fault concerns a material object, the evidence must be produced: a broken cup, a chipped plate; or if sloth is the sin, and the offender is guilty of not having leapt straight from bed at the summons, a pillow or a blanket must be exhibited as a symbol.* Unpunctuality for a meal is punished by making the offender go round the refectory with a little bell tied to her neck. The signal to begin eating is given by the Prioress, when in unison, as though at drill, the nuns throw back their long sleeves and unfold their napkins, fixing one corner to the table and the other to their chest, so that no

---

* This rule is frequently allowed to lapse in these days.

crumb may fall to the ground in transgression against their vow of poverty; any crumb which has fallen on the napkin must be picked up and eaten at the end of the meal, because Christ has said, "Gather up the fragments that remain that nothing be lost." Abstinence is permanent; meat never appears; all milk, butter, and eggs are likewise banished during Lent and on Fridays throughout the year, as well of course on the prescribed fast-days; on Good Friday only a little dry bread and water may be swallowed, not sitting at a table, but kneeling on the ground. No wonder that Teresa, who knew something about rough travel, had drawn a practical comparison: "What is our life of renunciation but one night to be spent in a bad hostelry? That is all."

But simplicity and even severity of life are things to which the most pampered may with good-will grow accustomed, whether they have been voluntarily incurred or no. When they are part of a chosen creed, a symbol of self-denial following an unspeakably greater example, every privation becomes a privilege, every loss a gain. The normal attitude to existence is indeed reversed, in the fundamental difference between the professed religious life and life as most of us lead it: not the avoidance of tribulation, but the welcoming of it as a God-sent increase to the value of the soul; not an occasion for bewailing but for rejoicing; poverty a boast, wealth a disgrace unless it might be devoted to the honouring of God; the greater the trial the greater the benefit. Taken from this point of view, the otherwise outrageous injustices imposed upon the long-suffering Job become intelligible. Teresa in her letters had never tired of telling her afflicted friars and prioresses how lucky they were, and how they ought to thank God for the grace of their sorrows. Thérèse could write of her unfortunate father that the three years he spent in a mad-house, struck with paralysis, as well as insanity, were the most agreeable and fruitful of her life, not to be exchanged for the most sublime ecstasies. And if what we should normally regard as the serious misfortunes are to be considered a cause for rejoicing, how insignificant though still welcome appear the minor hardships.

Furthermore, one should bear in mind the great comfort and support to be found in the life led by every unit in a community entirely dedicated to the same ideal, pursued with the same integrity. There is a certain and perhaps enviable simplicity in the mentality of most nuns which rejoices in the severe direction; the desire of the child for the strong hand and a competence more powerful than his own. The Catholic Church, after all, is the most totalitarian and intransigent of institutions, magnificently inelastic; and, as such, excellently suited to those whose temperament conforms to herd-obedience rather than to the querying recalcitrance of individualism. No room is provided for the refractory, but along the eternal corridor an endless succession of cells nine foot by nine for the docile. Acceptance is the keynote, and how delicious the repose when once acceptance has been accomplished! Only the misfit, the rebel, lonely in a world with different values, perhaps can estimate the consolation of finding himself at last with a company whose aims are entirely similar to his own. No longer a plant blown this way and that by the gale, his precarious roots loosened as he roughly sways, a strong stake now holds him fast, implacable wire engages his tendrils, and above his roots a mulch centuries-old in richness keeps him fed and cool. And as for the cell, it may be true that restricted measurements metaphorically harder than any concrete confine him, but there is no true duress here: the window is open over a landscape of unimaginable beauty, a liberty of spirit unknown even to the lark—nay, the very ceiling is off, open unlimited to a visionary height of his own and personal Heaven.

Thérèse never even mentions the minor hardships, although it was her custom to mention everything that crossed her mind. She who had described herself as so expansive, now submitted to the controlled recreation of a few moments conversation a day, preceded by a prayer that those moments should be well employed, within the scope of the subjects which may be discussed, interrupted three times by the castanets with their reminder of the Holy Presence, interrupted finally by a bell which stops you speaking, even in the middle of a word. The recreation room is completely denuded of furniture, for the rule of Carmel is that you must sit only on your heels, squatting on the floor. Thérèse never mentions this either, and it was only on her death-bed that she revealed verbally what she had suffered from the last and worst austerity: the cold. For Carmel forbids all heating. However bitter the winter, however damp, no concession is made even to a northern climate, with the exception of one single room which in the severest weather may be warmed up to 10° centigrade (50° Fahrenheit). Fingers which have grown so numb that they can no longer ply the needle may be held for relief to the comforting

I

stove. Thérèse, delicate and consumptive, was especially sensitive to cold. Even if she had warmed herself a little before going to bed— and we may be sure that she allowed herself this indulgence only when driven to it—she then had to go out again into the open, through the draughty cloister and down the icy corridors in order to regain her cell. The climate of Normandy runs to no such extremes as the climate of Castile; no knives of wind streak down from frozen sierras; but it can be cold, damp and foggy in that province of northern France which is not unlike the climate of England. Some nights when she could not sleep at all she lay shivering until the castanets made her throw off the poor covering of her blanket, but not until she was dying did they extract from her the pitiful admission, "What I have most suffered from physically in my religious life is the cold; I have suffered from it till I thought I should die."

If Thérèse could subjugate the flesh, accepting her trials not with any conscious martyrdom but gladly, there is no reason why we should dwell unduly on them. We may surmise that her battle lay rather with the subjugation of her own spirit. She had brought the essential part into the convent with her: the incandescent core which was her desire for the mystic union; she had brought also the message discovered in St. Paul's Epistle: the message of charity, perhaps better rendered as love. It remained now for her to work out her plan in detail, to find a comprehensive formula for her famous Little Way. Never to fail in the smallest particular; never the slightest relaxation of vigilance; the minutest slip on the self-imposed path to be instantly corrected and the balance restored; to act not dutifully but joyfully; to train the character by incessant practice until the eclipsing of self became second nature; it sounds obvious. Let any scoffer try the experiment conscientiously even for a week, even for a day, and find that the Little Way is neither so obvious nor so easy as it sounds.

The aims of Therese are far more comprehensible to the average mind than the mystical theology of Teresa. It is true that as a consequence of her intense love for Jesus she desired, and sometimes obtained, the mystic union; but in the other aspect of her faith reigned the ambition which may be put in the simplest and most childish words, "I will be good." The various States of Prayer of which one could make an almost genealogical table; the progressive Mansions

of the Soul; the difference between Bodily Sight and the Vision of
the Understanding; between the Understanding, the Will, and the
Memory; between Union and Trance; between Trance and Transport, between Raptures and Impetuosities; these things neither interested Thérèse nor played any part in her approach to God. It may seem
to some that hers was the less complex and more direct path to a
centre which others could reach only through the tortuosities and
checks of a maze. Why, we have already asked, enwrap in such intri-
cate technicalities an instinct which, in the last resort, is of the grandest
and most resplendent simplicity? The answer can be only, once again,
that of all human attributes the soul works in the most uncontrollable
of ways and that none can tell from which direction the order will
come. Thérèse, for example, gave herself up to Christ from the first
without hesitation or deviation, and all the rest naturally followed;
Teresa, impelled by very different motives, had to force herself into
His service, and, once there, travelled towards Him by very different
and far more disturbing means. To so profound a mystery, no inelastic rule can apply, and it pertained to the modest genius of Thérèse
to find her fulfilment in the words of the earliest nursery prayer:
"May it please God to make me good."

Pius XI put it neatly when he described her as "an exquisitely
delicate miniature of perfect saintliness."

VIII

ONE may, without thought of irreverence or flippancy, suggest that
as Teresa of Avila stands as the highbrow among saints, so does
Thérèse of Lisieux stand as the lowbrow; the Velasquez opposed to
the oleograph. Not accidentally have they been accorded the epithets
of "the great" and "the little." The Spaniard enjoyed the double
aristocracy of birth and intellect, the French girl belonged by birth
to the bourgeoisie and intellectually to the direct and simple. There
is a story of Teresa of Avila in conversation with a mother who wished
her daughter to be accepted as a candidate for Carmel. "She is very
devout," said the mother. "But has she brains?" asked the saint; "we

can teach people here to be devout, but we cannot give them brains."
Thérèse of Lisieux would never have said that. Not the inimitable
but the imitable saint, her faculty lay in symbolising and expressing
the daily need of ordinary folk; there was no originality in her
thought, no ambition in her behaviour beyond that supreme ambition, astounding in its audacity, its simplicity, and its execution, to
add herself to the Communion of Saints. The most remarkable thing
about the method she adopted (apart from her personal success in
carrying it out) was that nobody else had ever thought of formulating
it into a creed before. "In my Little Way," she said, "there is nothing
but very ordinary things; little souls must be able to do everything that I do." She had discovered, indeed, the Columbus' egg of
practical Christianity; "not to do extraordinary things, but to do
ordinary things extraordinarily well." The Little Way was a lane,
by-passing the main road of the heroic. It was a small orbit, but it
comprised nothing less than perfection. Unsensational, pierced by no
swords, no arrows, broken on no wheel, roasted on no gridiron,
she could have pursued her way as effectively "in the world" as
amidst the severities of Carmel. A jostling family, the cares of home,
the glad unspoken sacrifices of love, the anxieties of poverty, the
disappointments of competition, the betrayals of business, the mis-
understandings and misinterpretations of motive, the small exacer-
bations of human contact, all would come within the prescribed
quotidian system which was more than a system: it was a routine,
observed moment by moment. No need to go to Carmel in search
of an unjust Superior, of a sick and querulous old woman, or of a
nun who fidgeted with her beads in a manner to drive one mad. The
equivalent of these things could be found, and is to be found,
elsewhere.

There are many, indeed, amongst those living "in the world,"
subjected to its grind, its difficulties, its anxieties, its tangle of
ethics, its wearing exaction in the performance of duty, its clamour
for the sacrifice of self in the care of others, its demands upon our
sympathy and our practical helpfulness at cost to ourselves—many
who have no patience with the idea of the contemplative life. It
appears to them as a form of escape from reality; almost as a form of
self-indulgence, of selfishness, an evasion of responsibility, a withdrawal from the unpleasantness of a world which nevertheless is

everyone's charge to help within their own range to run. About the teaching or the nursing or the missionary Orders they feel differently. That is a thing which can readily be understood and respected, for it approximates more closely and even in a recognisably nobler degree to the calls made upon our own humanity and daily obligations. The applied heroism of a Father Damien or a St. Peter Claver is admirable to all. To the people of that mind—and they are in the large majority —our duty towards our neighbour is more urgent and immediate than our duty towards God; the one duty does not, and should not exclude the other; but God should be served through the medium of devotion to our human brotherhood, not through the quiet of a taper-lit chapel or the isolation of a cell. Estrangement from the burden of life is no part of our common citizenship; the prayers devoted to the evil of the general soul would be better translated into the care of the general body. To such arguments there is no comprehensive reply. There is only the reply that all spirits do not envisage the problem of life alike, and that of another's need and method of solution we can be no judge. The one place where we can never be is in another's mind, and the answer to our various enigmas is not single but multiple. If the wooden floor on which we tread with such confidence is not solid at all, but in truer fact a net of holes through which, did we but see it differently, we should fear to fall, how far more tentative should be our estimate of a region which does not even pretend to be visible or tangible! To each must be left the fulfilment of his own destiny; and it may well seem of supreme importance to some, through the graces specially accorded to them, to establish this rare communication between mankind, whose representatives they are, and its Creator. Possibly their nature is so constituted as to preclude any other form of service. Vocation is a word, and a beautiful one; and no word has ever come into existence in human speech save to express a reality which must be named. The reality comes first; the naming follows. Quarrel as we may with the apparent waste of energy, the waste of potential usefulness, the waste, as we see it, of virtue involved in a living burial; indignant though we may grow over the desertion and even the heartbreak of those who see themselves abandoned in a cold world as the door of the cloister shuts finally in their faces; irate though we may be over the loss of competence in a society which so grievously needs it, the loss of talent applied to cogent ends, the denial of usefulness where usefulness should surely be given—none of these arguments and resentments can or should apply if once we accept the to us strange but powerful principle that the mundane and material values can be turned utterly upside down.

The story of a Spanish girl may here not come amiss as an illustration. So far as we know, and it may certainly be accepted as a fact, Thérèse of Lisieux had never known anything, not even in the most virginal sense, of the exquisite though confusing delight of human passion. Her awakening to love had been reserved entirely for the celestial bridegroom. She had never dreamt of a nuptial chamber other than her cell; of a marriage-bed other than a board across two trestles in the lonely night. Such was not the case with Doña Casilda de Padilla. The only heiress to a rich and noble house, for her brother and elder sister had already renounced the world, she was hastily betrothed to a kinsman whom she loved with an affection beyond her years and with whom she would spend the day when occasion offered, to her great joy because she loved him so much. Yet at the end of every such day she fell into profound sorrow, thinking how the day was ended and how every other day must be ended in the same way. This gave her a sadness so great that she could not conceal it from her bridegroom, nor could she at first account for it though sensing her melancholy he pressed her to tell him the cause. The dress and ornaments of her rank, which after the ceremony of her betrothal they had begun to put upon her, gave her no pleasure such as was natural to a girl of her age, and gradually she began to realise that God meant to have her for Himself and was taking away from her the human love she felt. Her bridegroom was considerably older than she and took the matter seriously; moreover he found himself obliged to undertake a journey leaving his unsettled fiancée to her own devices. She had not the heart to speak to him at all plainly of her irresolution, but she did speak to her sister and mother, saying, if they thought her old enough to be married, how came it that they did not find her old enough to give herself to God? To cut the story short, she thought it wiser not to wait for his return, but under the pretext of going to visit her grandmother she made her way to a monastery, ridding herself of her dueña and attendants (for naturally no Spanish girl of her rank would have been allowed out unless heavily escorted) sending one of them to buy a bundle of faggots and another to fetch her a glass of water, while she evaded the others and broke into the monastery, weeping and imploring the Prioress not to send her away.

Her women lamented at the grating; the grandmother arrived, an uncle arrived, the bridegroom himself arrived, but nothing could move her. She would say only that she must work out her own salvation, adding for the consolation of the poor distraught man that she was leaving him only for God, and that he had no reason to complain of that, but "when she saw that he was not satisfied she arose and left him." It took an order from the King to remove her by force from that retreat. But, undefeated, she again gave her mother the slip one day when they had gone to Mass together and she had seen her mother safely into the confessional. Taking off her clogs,* putting them in her sleeve, and picking up her long skirts, Casilda ran in all haste back to the monastery pursued by her dueña who seeing herself outdistanced, called out to a man to stop her. The will of God, however, was such that the man found himself unable to move and Casilda shut the door behind her when the nuns immediately gave her the habit. Thus, for ever after rewarded with spiritual graces, she exchanged her "most rich and costly garments for the poor robe of serge."

If such urgency could be felt even by a girl in love, a girl to whom all the tenderest promises of the world were opening, a girl to whom renouncement meant not only the sacrifice of all sweet and tempting things,—love, children, home, riches, honour,—but also the painful obligation of wounding the heart of the man to whom she had given her own, how far more comprehensible becomes the determination of a heart-free Thérèse to seek the refuge of the cloister. The only person who could possibly be hurt was her old father; and, closely though she loved him, his claim upon her (had he chosen to make it) could not be allowed to stand between her and the reverberating call she heard from Christ. All other potential claims, of service to people she did not even know, were unformulated and, from her point of view, non-existent. The enclosed life gave the opportunity

* It is not surprising that Casilda should have removed her clogs (*chapines*) in order to run more freely, for these were sometimes of such a height that even walking in them was difficult.

for complete absorption, for the total gift of self, for the fusion she must experience if she was to fulfil her destiny at all. Like Casilda, only with fewer obstacles, she must work out her own salvation.

IX

ACTIVE though it was in some ways and not lacking in occupations, the life of Carmel was the contemplative life, and, as such, provided the perfect rounding-off for her philosophy. In order to amplify and clarify this point, it is necessary to expound something of the aims at Carmel and to show how they fitted in with her double intention of living the ultimate spiritual life and the faultless Christian life of daily contact. A manuscript of the thirteenth century declares that the life of Carmel has a double aim. The first, which may be attained by God's grace through our labours and the practice of virtue, brings to God a heart free from actual taint of sin, and is dependent upon the charity which covers all errors. The second aim is a gift of God, and consists in experiencing here on earth the force of the divine presence. It will thus be seen that although the first aim may be achieved by the exercise of our mortal will, the second is beyond our control and our only contribution can be a constant orientation of our desire towards the consummation. The rest must be left to God. Teresa of Avila herself had been well aware that not all her disciples would receive the final revelation but in spite of sacrifices and orisons would remain for ever on the secondary plane. She taught that the road to the true contemplation lay through the exercise of a giving and self-immolating love, but that the mystic union lay only in the background as a possible, miraculous, and infinite reward. St. John of the Cross put the same idea a little differently:

> Para venir a gustarlo todo
> no quieras tener gusto en nada.
> Para venir a poseerlo todo
> no quieras poseer algo en nada.

(In order to enjoy everything
    you require to find enjoyment in nothing.
In order to possess everything
    you require to possess nothing.)

He had enlarged also on the ideals which the soul should pursue:

Not the most easy but the most difficult.
Not the most savoury but the most insipid.
Not that which pleases but that which displeases.
Not to desire the greatest but the least.
Not to desire anything but to desire nothing.
To arrive at that which one ignores, one must follow the road where one ignores.
To arrive at that which one has not, one must follow the road where one has not.
To arrive at that which one is not, one must follow the road where one is not.
To obtain the All, one must abandon all,
And when you come to possess the All, hold it without wanting anything at all.

The premise of these ultimate values once accepted, there can be no escape from the logic of such an argument. The waters of mysticism are deep, and the peaks in its range of ambition high; confronted with such depth and such height, all else becomes insignificant. It is perhaps the most difficult of all subjects to discuss or interpret in words, since the essential privity eludes, the one thing needful is lacking, and words at best are only symbols of little meaning unless experience supplies the necessary element of recognition. In other and less abstruse fields even visual description can do no more than evoke a suggestion of the thing seen, yet in visual description some helpful element of familiarity is already present—a landscape, an effect of light, a flower, human features—but how far, even so, is the description removed from the reality! And if this be true, as it is undeniably true, then how incomparably harder to convey through the token-coinage of words any impression of a privity accorded to so few. The bank-note suggests little of the bars of gold buried in the cellars, or of the immense complication of weaving wealth in commerce and industry. As well attempt to explain the value of his penny to a beggar, or colours to a man born blind.

We are moving here upon a plane disconnected from earthly life.

Possibly the nearest approach to it is shared by the artist in his moments loosely called 'of inspiration,'

When the light of sense
Goes out, but with a flash that has revealed
The invisible world. . . .

for there is a greater resemblance between the creative artist and the mystic than between any other brands of human beings. It may be true of him that he walks then upon a tight-rope stretched between mundane and extra-mundane things; the comparison has often been drawn; but it must never be forgotten that although the inward sensation may be similar—that sense of being lifted out of self, exalted, filled with power, filled with a perception not blinding but revealing —it must never be forgotten that the aim is not consciously similar, not similar even in retrospect; unless, indeed, the pursuit of beauty runs a parallel path to the pursuit of God. As well it may. It is, at any rate, a desire for completion, a desire to resolve the confused and kaleidoscopic fragments into the entire pattern which must some-where exist; the desire to which some souls have given up their earthly lives. There is no such thing as an inherent mystery; there is only the mystery of a thing we but brokenly understand.

"There are moments, brief and unpredictable, when man has the sense of entering into immediate contact with an infinite Goodness . . . a semi-experimental perception of God, in very varying degrees of intensity and clarity. . . . No terms are of any use to render so new, so special, and so powerful an impression . . . an assurance given, a beam of light falling upon a living reality and illuminating it right down into its depths."

It has already been pointed out that in the higher mysticism the subject, one might almost say the victim, of ecstatic raptures accom-panied by physical phenomena preserves a cautious and mistrustful attitude: the sweats, the fevers, the pains, the tremblings, the loss of consciousness, the lightening of the body, are not manifestations to be proud of as signifying a divine grace, but rather to be evaded, regarded with suspicion, and if possible concealed. Curious, and even impressive in their departure from natural laws, though they may appear to the casual inquirer, to the initiated they appear as the secondary and inconsiderable phenomena of a lower plane of spirituality. The true and utterly purified communion of the spirit with God should be unaffected by bodily consequences, once it has passed beyond the first stage where the consciousness and even the senses are involved. In the Wisdom of Solomon, "The corruptible body presseth down the soul, and the earthy tabernacle weigheth down the mind that museth upon many things." St. John of the Cross, moving in his rarified air, dismissed such manifestations quickly and almost with a flick of contempt: the infirmities, sufferings, dislocation of the bones and other physical derangements were to him merely the result of ecstasies and raptures where the communications were not purely spiritual, for the sensual part of the soul is weak, without capacity for the strong things of the spirit. Basing themselves on this argument, it would be possible for the devotees of Thérèse of Lisieux to contend that her spirituality was of a higher order from the start than that of Teresa of Avila, since in her simplicity and openness of soul, her clear perceptivity, she had taken the short-cut to the goal where St. John's "ray of high contemplation" may strike the soul with its blinding, illuminating light. She had never been called upon to suffer the "physical derangements" as Teresa had suffered them. They were not wholly unknown to her, but it seems clear from her own account that they were neither frequent nor excessive. Teresa of Avila had been flung about by the Devil; he had crashed her against a wall; thrown her downstaris and broken her arm; her limbs had become frozen and rigid; she had felt herself lifted into the air "as though by an enormous eagle." Thérèse of Lisieux never underwent any trial approximating to this. How moderate, in comparison, is her narrative of one such incident, "I felt myself suddenly wounded by a shaft of fire so ardent that I thought to die of it . . . it seemed that an invisible force was plunging me wholly into fire. Ah, what a fire, what sweetness. . . . I seemed to be moving with a borrowed body, as though a veil had been thrown over all earthly things. But I was not burnt by a real flame." She refrained even from the temptation of indulging in physical mortifications and penances other than those already imposed upon her by the rule of her Order, preferring the mortifications which she could constantly impose upon her spirit, and it comes almost as a surprise to find that she once made herself ill by wearing a metal cross whose sharp points dug into her flesh. Gratuitous external heroism was of no value to her whose life was made up of another kind of oblation. To all ecstasies, she wrote, she preferred the monotony of an obscure sacrifice. Her piety, if such an expression may be permitted, kept its feet more firmly on the ground, and even in her intense sense of union with her Creator it is noteworthy that she seeks always to express her emotion in the terms which will bring herself and her audience down to the nearest possible approach of the human parallel. Using the word in its nicest sense, one might say that she sought always to *belittle*. It is Jesus who is her intimate; Jesus the intermediary; Jesus the tender, the compassionate; Jesus the link between our frailty and the too-august conception of God the Almighty. Teresa de Ahumada referred with a grand simplicity to "His Majesty," as one who is in the habit of frequenting Kings; Thérèse Martin prefers *le petit Jésus*, the Christ-child, the blond lover. Had not the Spaniard become, barely, "Teresa de Jesus," whereas the little French nun softened herself into "Thérèse de l'Enfant Jésus"?

One must ask oneself, though the question may horrify the devotees of St. Thérèse, was she a true mystic in the sense that Teresa of Avila and St. John of the Cross were true mystics? I think not. Not quite. It is true that she saw our Lady move and smile (though even in this case it must be taken into account that she lay at the time in a high fever and had a suggestive statue before her eyes); that she uttered prophecies, worked miracles, and felt the inner consciousness of Christ's presence within her. But was her experience of this grace not deliberate rather than supernatural? It was what she had always consciously desired; it had not assailed her inescapably and, as it were, from without as well as from within. It is easy to persuade oneself when all the heart and will are thrown into the striving. In saying this, we must not lose sight of the general agreement that union— the 'feeling' of presence—cannot be obtained by intentional effort, and it may be an apparent contradiction to suggest that Thérèse received the divine guest simply by opening the gates of her soul for His admission. Yet it must also be remembered that hysteria, which is closely associated with mysticism, in some cases takes the form of a transference of the love instinct, common to all but in some temperaments more urgent and consuming than in others. Psychologists go so far as to use the word erotomania. Not that this word must be taken in the defamatory sense. It may on the contrary be regarded as the purest possible desire for devotion to an ideal image, where "the soul is nothing but ardour and love," combined with a human longing for dependence, guidance, and protection which it naturally seeks in the most powerful conception known to it, the conception of the overwhelming God. Such a control relieves the fearful soul of vacillation and even of responsibility; problems are handed over into a stronger keeping; the mystery of existence is solved once and for ever; there is no conflict left save the conflict involved in the lively retention of the discovered truth; the answer to all questions is found. If this is the explanation of Thérèse's piety, even though like all explanations it may be only partially satisfying, it is not surprising that she should have evolved her own Little Way as her "first aim" through which she might hope eventually for an occasional visit snatched up into that region which is bathed in light. In its very smallness it was in a sense the natural outcome of her upbringing and her circumstances, though not of her temperament. Therein lay her heroism. She had not started on the Little Way equipped with a nature adapted to its exigences. Had unselfishness and self-effacement come quite naturally to her, as to some rare souls in the very air they breathe, there would have been less need to talk about it; it simply would not have occurred to her as anything unusual; and the Little Way might never have been so explicitly codified. But she was born self-willed, strong-headed, excitable, enthusiastic, spirited; it was not her instinct to give up to others or to give in. Asked once to give a definition of God's omnipotence, she had replied "It means that He does whatever He likes"—evidently an enviable status in her childish mind. On another occasion when she and her sister Céline were offered their choice out of a basketful of dolls' clothes and pieces of material and trimmings, all very desirable to the heart of a small girl, Céline modestly chose a roll of braid, but Thérèse grabbed and carried off the whole lot saying "I choose everything!" To us it is the natural reaction of the normal, avid child, but Thérèse saw it more symbolically. She observes that this incident of her childhood summarises her whole life, and that only later did the understanding come to her that in order to become a saint it was necessary to suffer much, to search always for perfection, and to forget oneself entirely; to choose everything, in fact, which God might send her. When the moment arrived for the Little Way to be put to the test, it would be seen how the patient training, the countless tiny inurements, the accumulation of resistance against the temptations of human weakness, would serve in the hour of trial like a well-disciplined army reliable in each of its component parts.

Thérèse Martin, before she became Thérèse de l'Enfant Jésus, had been groping towards the realisation of her ideal. There had been the incident of the shoes on Christmas-eve; there had been the sudden illumination of her personal interpretation of the Epistle to the Corinthians. Each one of us has known comparable moments of significance in other fields of life, not recognised perhaps at the time, but seen as an upstanding peak in a later and more distant survey of our hilly range. The curious thing is that Thérèse practically re-invented the doctrine of Carmel for herself. It is inconceivable that as a child she should have read the works of either St. Teresa or St. John of the Cross; their lives she surely read, or had read to her, but their deep and difficult metaphysical idiom would have been utterly beyond her understanding; she even remarks that "visible angels," by which she means her elder sisters, had been careful to choose books for her suited to the limited grasp of her years. It is probable that she had read *The Interior Castle* or had heard it read aloud in the convent refectory, since that was a work composed especially for the guidance of nuns in the difficult matter of prayer, and the same might apply to *The Way of Perfection* which of all St. Teresa's writings comes nearest to a statement of Thérèse's own principles; but, if so, she never mentions either of these works, and in any case she had evolved the basis of her own tenets before she ever reached the convent; yet she was only thirteen when she began to set herself a rule of life entirely consonant with St. John's and St. Teresa's precepts of love and abnegation leading to divine union, the *nada* and the *todo*, the nothing and the all. Even in minor matters Teresa had thrown off phrases very closely related to the Little Way: "In this most important matter (i.e. charity for our neighbours rooted in the love of God), we should be most vigilant in little things. . . . The Lord expects *works* from us. If you see a sick sister whom you can relieve, never fear losing your devotion; compassionate her; if she is in pain, feel for it as if it were your own. . . . This is the true union of our will with the will of God. If some one else is well spoken of, be more pleased than if it were yourself. . . . It is amusing to see souls who, while they are at prayers, fancy they are willing to be despised and publicly insulted, yet . . . if anyone unjustly accuses them of a fault, God deliver us from their outcries! Let those who cannot bear such things take no notice of the splendid plans they made when alone." Ever human, she had also written in a vein specially applicable to Thérèse, "Sometimes a trifling matter gives as much pain to one person as a heavy cross would cause another. Sensitive natures feel very keenly slight troubles." Yet at no time did Teresa become one of Thérèse's favourite authors. As a matter of fact she speaks but seldom of anything she read, and, since with our detailed knowledge of her it is fair to suppose that any strong literary influence would certainly have been recorded in her autobiography, it is fair also to suppose that no such influence came her way. It is therefore perhaps unjust to deny her any originality of thought, since unaided she arrived at her conclusions, not knowing that they had been reached before.

The pathos of it is that she loved reading but found little leisure for it; recognising it as a temptation to self-indulgence, she took the habit of restricting herself to a definite time, and on seeing that the hour was up would break off even in the middle of the most interesting passage. Remembering how Teresa in the stern Avila of her childhood had been brought up on the romances of chivalry and had even tried to write them herself in collaboration with her small brother, we find Thérèse making the admission that in certain *récits chevaleresques* she was unable to comprehend what she calls the positivity of life. In spite of this inborn aloofness from the life of action she cherished a great admiration for all patriotic French heroines, more especially for Jeanne d'Arc to whom she consecrated a long sequence of poems and also a prayer inspired by a picture of the soldier-saint. (How well one knows those representations of Jeanne! the one which Thérèse gazed at was doubtless very much to her taste.) Jeanne, of course, was not Sainte Jeanne to Thérèse, and it comes with the slight surprise of unfamiliarity to meet her in Thérèse's pages as merely the Venerable—a title which, with its other and more usual association with a dignified old age, strikes us as strangely unsuitable for that fiercely youthful virgin. One of the poems is devoted to an appeal for her canonisation. Innocent Thérèse! not all her gift of prophecy had shown her the illuminated splendour of St. Peter's, the crowds, and the processions, all in her own honour,

five years almost to the day after the elevation of Jeanne d'Arc.*
Nor, for all her prescience, did she foresee that some day her own
shrine or statue in the village churches as in the cathedrals of France
would enjoy the touching homage of a fresh because ever-renewed
bunch of flowers, whereas Jeanne the too-heroic would be left on
her pedestal, bearing a dusty standard above the withered sprigs of
bay or laurel. The rough little village of Domremy has something
to be thankful for: it has been spared the trashy shops and panoramas
of Lisieux. Even the soldiers of 1914–18 were to prefer the cameo-
saint to the saint who was slightly over life-size.

It cannot be claimed for Thérèse's poems that they have much
merit beyond their obvious sincerity, but her *Prière de la France à
Jeanne d'Arc*† may be quoted for its topical application. Some of her
devotees may even decide to regard it as prophetic, overlooking the
fact that it refers to the religious persecutions then prevalent in
France.

> Oh! souviens-toi, Jeanne, de ta patrie,
> Des tes vallons tout émaillés de fleurs.
> Rappelle-toi la riante prairie
> Que tu quittas pour essuyer mes pleurs.
> O Jeanne, souviens-toi que tu sauvas la France.
> Comme un ange du ciel tu guéris ma souffrance,
> Ecoute dans la nuit
> La France qui gémit:
> Rappelle-toi!

> Rappelle-toi tes brillantes victoires,
> Les jours bénis de Reims et d'Orléans;
> Rappelle-toi que tu couvris de gloire,
> Au nom de Dieu, le royaume des Francs.
> Maintenant, loin de toi, je souffre et je soupire.
> Viens encor me sauver, Jeanne, douce martyre!
> Daigne briser mes fers. . . .
> Des maux que j'ai soufferts,
> Oh! souviens-toi!

---

* Jeanne d'Arc was canonised on May 16th, 1920, Thérèse on May 17th, 1925.
† A literal translation will be found on p. 182.

LES BUISSONNETS, LISIEUX

ST. THÉRÈSE AT THE CONVENT OF LISIEUX

Je viens à toi, les bras chargés de chaînes,
Le front voilé, les yeux baignés de pleurs;
Je ne suis plus grande entre les reines,
Et mes enfants m'abreuvent de douleurs.
Dieu n'est plus rien pour eux! Ils délaissent leur Mère!
O Jeanne, prends pitié de ma tristesse amère!
Reviens, fille au grand cœur,
Ange libérateur,
J'espère en toi.

X

BUT what is to be said about her other writings, contained in that single, unique, and revealing document entitled The Story of a Soul (*Histoire d'une âme*)? True to her conviction that there were "some things which lost their scent when exposed to the air," she had not wanted to write it, and it was only in obedience to the wish of her Mother Superior, who at that time happened to be her sister Pauline, that she took up her pen to compose it under the difficult conditions of constant interruption arising from her other occupations and duties. In this, at any rate, she resembled Teresa who had suffered so much from interruptions that she was compelled to write late into the night when quiet had descended on the convent; but how insignificant appear Thérèse's interruptions compared with those of the busy woman who had not only her personal religious duties to attend to, but also the immense business involved in carrying out her foundations and the enormous volume of correspondence that rolled into all parts of Spain, into palace and convent, and into the New World itself, from her scurrying pen! But, balanced against this difference, Thérèse, who had not the intellectual strength of the Spaniard, suffered equally from the lack of spare time, of the time necessary for sustained concentration, a lack with which any writer will sympathise. Impossible to concentrate when irrelevant demands constantly break the spell. No wonder that her narrative is slightly incoherent, dodging backwards and forwards in its chronology as though the author had had no leisure to re-read and reassemble; that is of the smallest

K

importance. Indeed a great part of its charm lies in its very artlessness, its very breathlessness, as though she were anxiously in haste to empty her meaning on to the paper, to shake out the contents of her memory as it were, in compliance with her instructions and for the benefit of others. Once reconciled to her task, she had no doubt at all—and how right she was!—that although it was not to see the light until after her death, it would one day become of capital importance. Replying to her sister, who had bidden her to amplify an inadequate passage and who subsequently found her in tears, she exclaimed that it was so truly her soul; that those pages would do so much good in the world; that she felt convinced that everyone would love her. Her certainty on this subject seems to have equalled her certainty that she would become a saint. But, to say the worst at once, and to say it strongly, it must be admitted that much of *l'Histoire d'une âme* is intolerable to a different type of mind. The infantilism of Thérèse, the treacly dulcification, the reduction of the difficult to the easy, which inspire so enthusiastic a devotion and response in some, provoke an equivalent exasperation in others. The very sub-title on the first page gives a clue to what we may expect: The spring-tide story of a little white flower (*Histoire printanière d'une petite fleur blanche*).* There is, to some minds, something infuriating about the imagery and phraseology we encounter, as nauseating as a surfeit of marsh-mallows. The untranslatable words *mièvrerie* and even *niaiserie*, words which one of her most devoted admirers among her countrymen has not hesitated to apply, can in English be rendered only by such adjectives as sugary, namby-pamby, and silly. We are far indeed from the metaphysical splendours of Teresa of Avila, far from the reptiles and the brilliant diamond larger than the whole world; far from the dark luminosity of St. John of the Cross; as far removed as are the plaster figures of saints from the splendours of art once lavished upon the honouring of God. Strange it is that religion which once inspired the noblest examples of man's creation, should find expression also in the tawdry and the tinsel; the artificial flowers; the gaudy gilding; the figures coloured in the lollipop pinks and blues; simpering vulgarity mixed with the insipidity of bad senti-

* This is doubtless responsible for the sobriquet of "The Little Flower," by which St. Thérèse is frequently known in English, though, so far as I am aware, in no other language.

mentalism. Where are the jewelled windows of Bourges and Auxerre?
the embroidered vestments of Peregrino Tibaldo, the treasures of
many a Spanish sacristy? the frescoes of Assisi, of Padua, of the Sistine
Chapel? the angels of Fra Angelico? the sly and subtle images of
Leonardo? the bronzes of Ghiberti? Those things were fine and
rich and strong. The question arises, did they reflect the general taste
of their day, were those generations truly of a different stamp? or
was there always the simpler cruder taste whose gimcrack owing
to its very fragility has long since perished without trace? We have
no means of knowing, though the absence of cheap and standardised
ornaments must have gone far towards hindering the disfigurement
of church and side-chapel by untutored if loving hands. Lisieux
itself, although it has escaped the worst blemishes of Lourdes, has
now transformed one of its streets into a series of shops where the
tourist may purchase for a few francs such objects as inkstands in
oxidised *art nouveau*, dominated by a figure of Thérèse, medallions
and *bijoux Fix* by the thousand, coloured lithographs, miniature
reproductions of the marble group at Les Buissonnets, and tinted
sprays of Les Roses de Lisieux supplied also in garlands at 35 francs
the yard. There is also a gallery showing scenes from the life of
Thérèse in waxwork, life-size; the visitor walks round, following all
the events from the six-year-old Thérèse discovering the T in the
sky to the last death-bed scene in the infirmary, and emerges again
to meet with the pinchbeck in its inexhaustible supply.

It is perhaps inevitable that such taste should appeal to the simple
and childish populace, and even to the humbler kind of priest as well
as to his congregation. Children delight in raw colours and flashy
ornament; they respond to ingenuity exemplified by the painted
tin flower more excitedly than to the real flower itself; and not all
priests could qualify for the intellectual standard of the Society of
Jesus however valid a passport they may carry to the frontier guarded
by St. Peter. Of such may be the Kingdom of Heaven, and to this
touching company Thérèse de l'Enfant Jésus with her Little Way
certainly belonged. Her spiritual attainments might rival those of
her high Castilian namesake, but in her daily and vernacular exposition
she spoke to and for the many, the unpretentious men and women
who were troubled, who were confused, who knew nothing of the
hierarchy of prayer or its seven mansions, nothing of contemplation

acquired or infused; who merely wanted "to be good," who wanted an intelligible interpretation of the inklings they felt within them; who in fact wanted a kindergarten, introductory to the immense and difficult region of intimation they sensed as lying beyond.

It was not only that Thérèse's teaching was comprehensible and above all applicable, even in a modified degree, to ordinary life; it was also that her language, her instances, and her metaphors echoed the recognisable experience within the range of all. Her metaphors could at times be very charming in their freshness and naïvety; thus, speaking of her Little Way which is to be "so straight, so short, so novel," she observes gravely that she is living in a century of inventions, when it is no longer necessary to climb the staircase step by step; in the houses of the rich, she says, it is advantageously replaced by a lift (*un ascenseur*), and she, Thérèse, must find a lift to take her up to Jesus. The kaleidoscope with which she played as a child affords her another illustration: investigating its works, she discovered that her pretty patterns came from nothing but irregular bits of paper and wool, but ah! there was a further discovery: a three-sided mirror down the centre, the Holy Trinity of course, turning the meaningless jumble into beauty. She could display some humour too—she had been a merry child—and cured a novice of her too-ready tears by making her hold a shell up to her eyes to catch them. After this, the novice relates, whenever she felt inclined to cry she armed herself with the pitiless instrument, but was kept so busy chasing from one eye to the other that she quite forgot the reason of her sorrow in laughter.

So far so good, but with the best will in the world we must acknowledge that Thérèse sometimes overshot the mark when her naïvety toppled off its precarious knife-edge into the ludicrous. At those times, while according her all the simplicity of which the purest and most child-like soul is capable, one is forced to reverse one's opinion and declare that she can have possessed no humour whatsoever. Two instances shall suffice. The first concerns the *lettre de faire part*, in this case an announcement of marriage, which she composed for the entertainment of the other novices. The opening sentences ran as follows:

"God Almighty, Creator of heaven and earth, sovereign Dominator of the world, and the Most Glorious Virgin Mary, Queen of the celestial court, are pleased to inform you of the spiritual marriage of their august Son, Jesus, King of Kings and Lord of Lords, to little Thérèse Martin, now Lady and Princess of the realms brought her as her dowry by her divine Spouse."

The second instance concerns the coat-of-arms which she designed for herself and Jesus. It is most elaborately drawn and blazoned; two shields, side by side, are surmounted by the respective initials J.H.S. and M.F.T. (Marie Françoise Thérèse). The Holy Child lies on a

pillow, playing with a bunch of grapes which represents Thérèse's own desire to offer herself first as a plaything to His every whim and then as a means of quenching His thirst. On Thérèse's shield amongst other symbols appears the inevitable little flower turning up its face to some rays of light. Under the legend, "Days of grace accorded by the Lord to his little wife," are listed the significant dates in her short life: Smile from the Holy Virgin, 13th May 1883; First Communion, 8th May 1884; Confirmation, 14th June 1884; Conversion, 25th December 1886; Audience with Leo XIII, 20th November 1887; Entry into Carmel, 9th April 1888.

No doubt that the composition of this design was undertaken by Thérèse with the utmost sincerity and emotion, mingled with an all too playful daring of inventiveness. It really meant something to her, as she carefully drew and painted, and made out the explanatory notes, and then put it away between the pages of the *Histoire d'une âme* where it was found after her death. It is impossible to laugh at the innocent game; one marvels only that such *niaiserie* and such heroic seriousness could live together in the same soul.

Equally difficult of acceptance to the critical mind is the constant betrothal-bridal motif, not, certainly, peculiar to Thérèse among pious women, but surely pushed by her to the limits of our reasonable endurance. Teresa of Avila herself had shared the feeling; she has constant references to this theme. But, even so, there is a difference between her impassioned address and Thérèse's sentimentality; her love is of a more adult nature; she speaks as a woman, with a woman's knowledge, not as a maiden bewildered by her first falling in love. Moreover she can go to the length of apologising for her analogy: "Though but a homely comparison, yet I can find nothing better to express my meaning than the Sacrament of Matrimony though the two things are very different." It may be objected also, as a comparison not a contrast, that Teresa had cherished a Christ-doll which she carried with her on her journeyings, and that Thérèse would much have liked a doll also; it was just the thing to suit her fancy. But we may surmise that Thérèse's doll would have been dressed in white muslin tricked out with blue ribbons, whereas Teresa's doll belonged rather to the race of processional images, borne rocking shoulder-high on feast days through the streets of Spanish cities, in all the rigid gorgeousness of brocade and jewels: she had that tradition behind her, a tradition of high ceremony not of the nursery. The century and the country may possibly affect the judgment, but there does seem a real difference between Thérèse's rather skittish armorial designs at Lisieux in the 1880's and the commanding figure in the curtained waggon, clasping the stiff stylised puppet with savage vigilance across the wildernesses of Spain.

Thérèse never sees herself in this quasi-maternal protective role; she sees herself only as the fiancée, the bride, the toy. "I told the child Jesus," she says, "not to make use of me as a valuable toy which children are content to look at without touching it, but as a little ball of no price, which He could throw on the ground, kick with His foot, make a hole in, and either leave in a corner or press to His heart if that was agreeable to Him. In a word, I wanted to amuse the little Jesus and to give myself up to all His childish whims. . . . In Rome, He did make a hole in His little toy; no doubt He wanted to see what was inside it; and then, satisfied with His discovery, He let fall His little ball and went to sleep." She is not always a ball, even a ball "punctured with innumerable pin-pricks"; sometimes she is a little paint-brush, used to fill in the details on the general canvas; sometimes a little basin filled by God with good things for kittens to come and eat; often, of course, she is His little floweret (*Sa petite fleurette*), and even on occasion He offers her a nice little salad (*une bonne petite salade*), astringent because full of vinegar and spice, but lacking oil. It is all very homely; it is all drawn from the nursery and the kitchen of Les Buissonnets. Whipping-tops, ninepins, dirty pinafores, and rumpled hair are also pressed into illustrative service. She leaves a letter purporting to come from *ton petit frère Jésus* in the cell of a novice, asking her to exchange the game she has hitherto played for one that He now prefers. She taught the novices how not to be greedy by telling them a story of her own invention, which must have appealed particularly to those French girls who knew what cooking meant. "I pretend that I am at Nazareth in the house of the Holy Family. If I am offered salad, cold fish, wine or anything else with a strong taste, I give it to the good St. Joseph. To the Holy Virgin I give the warm dishes and the ripest fruits; and I give the Child Jesus the feast-day dishes, especially soup, rice, and jam. But if I am offered a bad dinner, I say gaily to myself, It's all for you to-day, my little girl!" Thérèse took what she knew, and as it happened to be what millions of other people also knew, it supplied a very usefully intelligible link between common humanity and the higher revelation.

> We'll see Him take a private seat
> And make His mansion in the mild
> And milky soul of a soft child.

Crashaw wrote this of Teresa, but how far more applicable it is to Thérèse.

The fiancée and the bride are usually treated by her in equally tender terms. She is invariably the little fiancée, and the bridal day when she finally takes the veil evokes a veritable rhapsody of italicised littleness. It was "the *little* Holy Virgin presenting her *little* flower to the *little* Jesus. Everything was *little* on that day," she says, but adds "except the graces that I received, except my peace and my joy in contemplating the beautiful stars of the firmament that evening, in the knowledge that I should soon take flight to heaven to unite myself to my divine Husband in eternal happiness."

It would be but a shallow spirit, however, which peered exclusively and with a dismissive irritation at Thérèse's mannerisms, for the tough core of heroism is there, even if it must be disinterred from under layers and layers of cotton wool. The heroism of course consisted in apparently little things, but little things in such multitude, in such accumulation, that they finally fitted her for the physical martyrdom she was later called on to endure. Long since, she had trained herself in the habit of never complaining, of never explaining when unjustly accused, of never giving way to impatience if she found her possessions appropriated by others, of choosing always the irksome task and persuading herself that it was pleasurable. Was she unfairly reproached for leaving a vase in a dangerous position? she made no reply, except to promise to be less careless in future. Was there an aged, infirm, and querulous nun? she would take her under her charge, and with unstinted patience would end by pleasing her when all the others had failed. Was she harshly treated by the Mother Superior and the Mistress of the novices? she accepted their severities without a murmur. Scolded for overlooking a spider's web in the cloisters, scolded for pulling up weeds in the garden, which nevertheless she was doing by order, her sensitive nature suffered but she would not allow herself to protest. Was she tempted to seek the company of her own two sisters among the nuns? she denied herself this indulgence, she to whom the affection of her family had meant so much. One of her worst trials came from the proximity at prayers of the fidgety nun who never stopped rattling her rosary or rustling something or other; Thérèse, who was endowed with exceptionally keen hearing, thought that probably no one but herself noticed it, but to her it was a distraction and a torture she could not express in words. She longed to turn her head with a reproachful look—a sufficiently mild rebuke, one would imagine, administered by one who was literally bathed in sweat from annoyance—but instead of this, and instead of trying to ignore the sounds, which would in fact have been impossible, or so she says, she set herself to listen attentively "as though the disagreeable little noise had been a ravishing concert." In the same way she overcame her very comprehensible dislike of having dirty water splashed into her face at the laundry wash-tub, and, instead of wiping it away, pretended to herself that she enjoyed it, with such goodwill that at the end of half-an-hour she really believed that she had acquired a taste for "this novel form of aspersion."

She had always liked pretty objects, or, at any rate, objects which she considered pretty; but she persuaded herself into a liking for objects which were not only ugly but also inconvenient in use. Thus, the water-jug in her cell had pleased her by its comeliness, but so well had she trained herself that she could actually rejoice when it was removed and replaced by one that was both coarse and chipped. Perhaps unconsciously, she was living up to Teresa's regulation that if a nun should be observed to like one thing better than another, it should at once be taken away from her.

It seems that she extended her rule of forbearance in a mysterious manner even to those beyond her immediate reach. On hearing one day that her sister Céline, who was still 'in the world,' proposed to attend a party with her cousins, Thérèse entered into a state of terrible distress and with many tears besought our Lord to prevent Céline from dancing. It fell out as she desired. Céline, habitually a graceful dancer, found herself unable to execute a single step; and, more remarkable still, her partner was likewise incapacitated from doing anything but walk, "most religiously with mademoiselle, to the great surprise of the entire company, after which the poor gentleman stole away (ce pauvre monsieur s'esquiva) in shame without daring to reappear during the rest of the evening." Teresa, on the other hand, had often spent the recreation hour dancing to her own tambourine in the cool of the Spanish evening, accompanied by the castanets of her nuns.

All the same, we should not suppose that Thérèse's convent life was wholly without its innocent pleasures. There was a sweetness in her nature which had always made her turn to birds and flowers, and one of her greatest renunciations on entering Carmel had been the thought that she would no longer be free to run in the meadows gathering her nosegays. To her great delight she was not called upon wholly to bear this privation, but was given the charge of an altar which she might decorate with the cornflowers, poppies, and marguerites supplied in sheaves by the faithful. They were the wild flowers of the countryside, and had always had her preference. As for the birds, with memories of her canary and her linnet in her mind, she made it her business to collect any dead one she found lying on the ground and to give it gentle burial in a tiny cemetery in a corner of the garden. It does not sound a very cheerful occupation, perhaps, but it appears to have afforded her great satisfaction. The snow was another pleasure of which the enclosed life could not deprive her. Despite her dread of the cold, she had always loved snow even as a child: perhaps, as she remarks, because of her birthday being in January, she was herself a "little flower of winter." But now her joy in it was doubled, for she could reflect that no mortal lover had the power of releasing a single snowflake from Heaven in order to charm his beloved.

On three occasions in the year, too, the convent rule was relaxed in order to give its inhabitants, especially the young novices, an opportunity for the outlet of their repressed high spirits. After all, they were but of the age of schoolgirls, and moreover it may be true to say that in such communities, deprived of all natural contacts with life, forced into what is, humanly speaking, an unnatural mode of existence, privy indeed to an enlightenment and a concentration of purpose unknown to those living in the jostle of a confusing world, but singularly unacquainted with the releasing activities of human energy, there exists an atmosphere of innocent and immature fun, readily satisfied by elementary jokes and accompanied by ripples of guileless laughter. Teresa, who knew her daughters inside out and had no illusions about their frailties innocuous or otherwise, had recognised in her wisdom that a little diversion was desirable to relieve the tension of high-minded living. We remember that when she had retired to her cell intending to devote herself for the rest of the evening to prayer and meditation, she had good-humouredly laid aside her books in response to a gay and somewhat imperious summons to come down and entertain the sisters with her conversation; and, as we know, far from pulling a long face at dancing, she even joined in it herself, standing on no dignity, for, with all her severity, she was the least glum or pompous of Prioresses. It was thus the custom of Carmel to allow three annual days of relaxation, once on the Feast of the Holy Innocents (December 28th), once on the feast of the Holy Name, a few days later, and once on the feast of St. Martha (July 29th). The feast of the Innocents, appropriately enough, is given up to the novices who become the star-turn (*vedette*) of the day. From morning onwards, the constitution of authority is turned upside down; in all matters except those relating to the holy offices, the heads of the community, Prioress, Sub-prioress, and Mistress of the novices, lay down their rank and are replaced by playful young substitutes who make the most of their brief reign. What matter though their election be slightly faked in order to fall on those who can best be trusted not to abuse their responsibility? Considerable licence is allowed, and the superiors take it in good part when, according to custom, a little harmless fun is indulged in at their expense. Laughter goes unchecked, the fresh laughter of young girls over all the muddles and upsets which they deliberately provoke; work is abandoned; no one darns, no one scrubs floors, stands over the steam of the wash-tub, or sweeps the dust out of the cloister. The crowning festivity comes in the evening, and has been surreptitiously prepared on the previous day. It is a kind of charade, full of references to the life of Carmel, performed by the novices for the benefit of their elders; they have been allowed to ransack cupboards and wardrobes for any scrap of material they can find—and in that establishment vowed to poverty the haul is pitiable enough: a few tatters stitched on to the brown habit, but the spirit is what counts, and to their restricted standard of jollity the entertainment seems as rollicking as a carnival.

The next celebration, in honour of the Holy Name, is more soberly conducted and consists principally in a profound concentration on the aspect of Christ as a baby; the only treat, in the mundane sense of the word, is a certain suspension of the rule of silence.

But in high summer towards the end of July the novices again have things all their own way. It is the feast of St. Martha, that pleasant homely character who, with a large bunch of keys hanging at her girdle and a ladle in her hand, bustles forward as the patroness of all good housewives. (It is a little surprising to find her accompanied also by a captive dragon, which she is said to have acquired at Marseilles.) This day very suitably is devoted to the sole annual holiday of the *sœurs converses*, lay-sisters, of whom there are three or four in a Carmelite convent, and whose normal duties include all the cooking, the care of the garden and the poultry-yard, as well as the stitching of the *alpargates*; in short, always bent over some labour, on July 29th they may stand upright, stretch their backs, and take a day's rest while younger hands perform their duties for them. They are made the heroines of the occasion; specially composed verses are recited in their honour; flowers are set before their places at the dinner-table; they are assiduously waited on, and the improvised young cooks vie with one another in the preparation of dishes which, without infringing the rules of abstinence or depleting too extravagantly the convent's meagre stocks, shall yet bring some treat and variation into the monotonous bill of fare. Humble *sœurs converses*! throughout the year they have risen an hour earlier than the rest of the convent, they have toiled unceasingly, murmuring their prayers as they laboured; they have been orderly and frugal; it is fitting that the good St. Martha should remember them once a year and bring them repose.

Thérèse does not refer to these recreations, though there can be no doubt that whether as a novice, a nun, or as Mistress of the novices (for, in spite of her youth, she rose to this position) she fully enjoyed this authorised pleasure, entering into the fun as gaily as ever she had played her own games at Les Buissonnets. She had not been very successful at joining in the games of her school-fellows, but then they had teased her and laughed at her; here, within the walls of Carmel, it was different, it was like a family despite the rubs and injustices, and underneath it all lay the common centralisation on the same great purpose. That could never be lost sight of, even in the midst of a frivolity which the Superiors in their wisdom had ordained. But there can be equally little doubt that, after her compliance, she returned with thankfulnes to the silence and solitude of her cell, where she might pursue undisturbed the trains of thought and meditation which so continuously occupied her mind. They were dreadful enough, some of those hours, for it must not be supposed that the life of "the little saint" was made up entirely of the little things, whether onerous or agreeable. Like all of her kind, she was familiar with the terrible spiritual crises described by that beautiful phrase, "the dark night of the soul." It seems strange, and a truly great mystery, that those who have so clearly heard a call to the reversal of the wordly order of things, who have been so intensely persuaded of the omnipresence and demands of God, who have so rapturously basked in the warmth of divine love as they understand it, should yet be subjected to those periods of doubt, aridity, and despair when the entire significance of their discovery seems withdrawn from them. Since the Christian mystics are so prone to make use of the imagery and even the phraseology of human love when speaking of the love of the soul, it may be permitted to reverse the simile and to consider for a moment how improbable would be a comparable occurrence in the love of the heart. Jealousy, quarrels, and suspicion, those human failings, we may disregard since they have no counterpart in man's striving towards God; but is it conceivable that a happy love, a love fulfilled and reciprocated, a love which is the finding of the perfect complement, should undergo such intervals of utter blank, when the thought or presence of the beloved should bring no stirring, no excitement, no transport, no response, no glow? It is not conceivable. A sense of unworthiness possibly, but never a total deadness of the fibres, an inability to blow a spark from the apparently extinguished fire. The reply may be that God is not always manifest even to the most ardent seeker; not manifest in the sense that the hand may be clasped, the body embraced, and the voice heard in its accents of reassurance. Theologians hold that this periodic drying-up of the spirit is sent as a test from God in order to show it that nothing but a desolation remains, a vacuum, once God is absent; that the spirit in itself and by itself is nothing. Teresa, herself a doctor of theology, had declared that God often temporarily withdrew His favours and that no more was needed to prove to us in a very short time what we really are. A salutary spiritual chastisement at the hand of God would seem indeed the only way for the worshipper to explain the discrepancy between the benevolence of the God of love and the obduracy of the God of wrath. The affliction of temporal misfortune, with its lesson not to set store on false values, may be understood; but this bereavement in the well-intentioned soul, desirous only of the utmost closeness with its Creator, is one of the major mysteries. Why should He who wishes to draw souls closer to Himself, elect to punish so cruelly those very ones who ask no better than to dwell constantly in the light of His presence and to sacrifice themselves utterly to His service? Why this hideous forfeiture, reducing St. Francis de Sales to the cry "Although He should kill me, I will trust Him"? The lover of God has to take much on trust; the conviction and the conflagration must come from within the soul; and at times the soul flags; the effort is too great; it demands a respite; but during that respite what torments arise, what fearfulness, lest the treasure should be lost for ever, what sense of guilt and betrayal, what anguish of deprivation, what extinction of the vital light! Teresa said that the mind felt then as if it never had thought of God nor ever would be able to do so, and that when men spoke of Him, they seemed to be talking of some person heard of long ago. Strangest of all, perhaps, is the persistence which, despite the deadness of spirit, the abysmal blank, the inability to pray save with the lips, nay, sometimes even the positive disinclination to prayer, still holds the unfeeling soul fast in its determination not to relinquish the thing it paradoxically no longer apprehends.

Something of this unexaggeratable anguish breaks from time to time through the rambling and almost chatty pages of the *Histoire d'une âme*. The prattle ceases, and in its place comes a cry as poignant as the cry of an animal trapped in the night. It is the echo of "My God, my God, why hast Thou forsaken me?" "One must pass through this martyrdom in order fully to understand it. . . . It was night, deep night, complete desertion, a veritable death. . . . Bitterness filled my soul to the brim. . . . I passed through the most furious tempest of my whole life. . . ." The practical difficulties put in the way of her admission to Carmel were as nothing compared with "this terrible disease of scruples," this doubt lest for all her struggles she might after all have been mistaken in her vocation. Nature itself, she said, seemed to accord with her sorrow: the sun was hidden, rain fell in torrents; she had noticed it always at those times. She could sympathise with the agonised anxiety of St. Joseph and the Holy Virgin as they sought throughout the streets of Jerusalem for the missing Child. She knew that Jesus was there somewhere, peacefully asleep, but how could He be seen through such obscurity? If only a thunderstorm would break, to cut the clouds with a shaft of lightning! That sense that there somewhere, just round the corner, but beyond reach, veiled, inaccessible, lay all comfort, all refreshment, was more deathly than death itself, for it carried with it the devilish suggestion of one's own mistake.

No amount of recurrent personal experience, nor the recorded and similar experience of other people, can alleviate the soul in such accesses of despair.

XI

OBEDIENCE of course was the prime and absolute rule, in small things as in great. Teresa sometimes had amused herself by testing the obedience of her nuns with ludicrous orders to see how far she could go without her authority being questioned. Thus one day in the refectory she was given a cucumber for her portion, very small and rotten within. Pretending not to notice, she called a sister to her and bade her go plant it in the garden. "She asked me whether it was to be planted endways or sideways. I told her sideways. She went and planted it, without thinking that it could not possibly fail to die." This was harmless enough, but Teresa realised that under such acceptance of discipline it was not always wise to speak in jest. She had seen her own Prioresses get themselves into awkward situations in such a way. The Prioress at Toledo, looking at a pond in the garden, wondered out loud what would happen if she told a certain sister to throw herself in; the sister overhearing this, was immediately in the water, and so much wetted that she had to be sent to change her habit. This same Prioress, reproving a nun, told her she had better put her head in the well and there think of her sins, and such was the haste of the culprit to obey that, had they not gone quickly after her, she would have jumped right in and been drowned. It was very necessary, as Teresa said, for Prioresses to be cautious in dealing with souls whom they already knew to be obedient, otherwise they might find themselves in the position of the Prioress who, on being shown a very large worm by one of her daughters, replied "Go and eat it." Only through the surprise of the cook on seeing a nun frying a worm, was the consummation prevented.

Thérèse no more than any other devout nun would ever have dreamt of going against the wishes of her superiors, but a wistful desire did come her way: she had heard that two Carmelites were needed for the convent at Hanoï in Indo-China. Had not Noah dispatched a dove from the Ark, and why should not she, Thérèse, also fly forth bearing the olive-branch towards those infidel shores? It occurred to her that her life at Lisieux was too soft, surrounded as she was by the love of her sisters both natural and spiritual, whereas by transporting herself to a foundation where she would be totally unknown, she might gain the benefit of suffering the pains of exile. But it was already apparent that another and longer journey awaited her, not into exile indeed, but into the haven she logically longed to reach.

A Good Friday had brought her the first indication of the joy in store. It so happened that she had been feeling in unusually good health and had gone all through Lent observing the strictest fast without ill-effects, and it was much to her disappointment that she had not been allowed to keep vigil by the Sepulchre for the whole of the Thursday night. It was midnight when she returned to her cell, and no sooner had she put out her lamp and laid her head on the pillow, than she became aware of a flood surging into her mouth, causing her to think that she was about to die and consequently filling her with bliss. A natural curiosity made her want to relight her lamp, but true to her principles she suppressed the impulse and went quietly to sleep until morning. When the castanets sounded, she awoke, filled with the conviction that she had something joyful to learn; carried her handkerchief to the window, and found it soaked in blood.

So well did she conceal this happening from her companions and her superiors, that she was allowed without question to carry out all the obligations imposed upon her by that most tragic of the Church's holy days. The Prioress must have been either singularly unobservant or singularly unsympathetic, compared with the little novice who found Thérèse cleaning the windows, and, noticing her livid face and obvious exhaustion, implored her to ask to be relieved of her task. Thérèse, of course, forbade her to say a word, remarking that she could well put up with a little fatigue on that day when Jesus had endured so much. Even her own sisters knew nothing of her condition until a year had passed.

She had been delicate from birth, nearly losing her life on several occasions during her babyhood and childhood; moreover her family history from a medical point of view could scarcely have been more deplorable. She had lost two brothers and two sisters, one of them certainly through consumption; she had lost an aunt through consumption; her mother had died of cancer, and her father was now paralytic and mad. It was not a good record. Oddly enough, and unlike Teresa of Avila some three hundred and ten years earlier, she had escaped very lightly from a similar epidemic of influenza which devastated France and found its way into the Carmel of Lisieux in 1891, when all the nuns save two fell ill and several died. Nevertheless, while still possessing her ordinary state of health, she had confided her prescience of death to an aged nun in whose discretion she could trust. "I shall die soon," she had said; "I don't say that it will be within a few months, but within two or three years at most." Her prophecy proved to be correct. Within two years and five months she was dead.

Thérèse had always been physically courageous; as a child she had enjoyed thunderstorms and in her religious life she never allowed fits of giddiness or blinding headaches to interfere with her duties. She had concealed them, as she had concealed the digestive troubles which were not improved by fasting or by the lean diet of Carmel. But there was now no question of concealment: she was attacked by tuberculosis of the lungs, accompanied by violent and repeated haemorrhages and a continuous dry cough. She could be observed painfully mounting the stairs towards her cell, obliged to pause on each step to regain her breath—not so very many years ago she had also paused on each step, calling "Maman! maman!"—so exhausted on arrival that it sometimes took her an hour to undress. Her condition at last realised, she was subjected to various treatments such as frictions, leeches, and cauterisation, a painful process which involved stabbing her with hot irons, but the doctor himself put little faith in his remedies, remarking that although he could not cure her, that soul was never made for earth. The less observant members of the community, evidently, did not all share the doctor's opinion of her saintli-

L

ness, for one day Thérèse overheard a nun talking in the kitchen and saying, "Sœur Thérèse de l'Enfant Jésus is soon going to die, and I really wonder what our Mother will find to say about her after her death. She will find herself in rather a difficulty, for although that little sister is amiable enough she has never done anything worth talking about." Her remark referred, of course, to the Carmelite custom by which the Prioress sends a biographical notice on any deceased nun to all convents of the Order. It would be interesting to know by how many years that nun survived St. Thérèse; it is quite possible that she may still be alive to-day.

By the end of Lent 1897 it became clear that the end could not be many months off, but to Thérèse herself it approached much too slowly. Characteristically, she compared herself to a child who has been promised a cake, always withdrawn when he tries to take it. Characteristically also she begged to be left in her cell instead of going to the more comfortable infirmary where her cough would disturb other people. Shut alone into her cell, she could not be heard. She would drag herself into the garden to enjoy the spring sunshine, then the warmer sunshine of May and June, but by July she was compelled to leave her wretched cell for the last time and resign herself to entering the infirmary. They kept on asking her if she feared death, an idle question. "I am as gay as a chaffinch," she wrote in a farewell letter to her uncle and aunt, "except when I have fever, but luckily that is only at night, when all chaffinches are asleep, their heads under their wings!" The door of her sombre prison was opening, she said; but by a cruel trial the darkness of the soul which, like all her kind, she had so often had to combat, returned to her at times, when she tossed upon her bed tempted to question whether God indeed loved her, begging them all to pray for her, imploring the Sister to throw holy water over her face for the Devil was around her, tormenting her, holding her down with an iron hand, impeding her from prayer. "Oh," she cried, "how one ought to pray for the dying! if only people knew!" At moments she seemed driven almost out of her mind by these mental sufferings; at other times she would regain all her confidence and serenity which no physical suffering, however atrocious, could shake.

"You are in great pain just now, are you not?"

"Yes, but I have so longed for it."

She spoke of her life after death. "I shall send down a rain of roses," she said. "I feel that my mission is about to begin, my mission of making others love God as I love Him, of giving my Little Way to souls. I want to show them the little methods which I have found so perfectly successful. I want to spend my heaven doing good on earth," but interspersed with such prophecies and amidst the distraction of her mortal pain she still did not fail to pursue those little methods of self-suppression. In a raging fever one night, and longing above all things for a cooling drink, the Sister brought her a hot-water bottle and iodine to rub on her chest. It was the height of summer, and poor Thérèse who had felt the cold so bitterly addressed a mental reproach to Jesus, "Bear witness," she said to Him, "I burn, and they bring me fire and more heat instead of half a glass of water! But I am glad to lack my necessity, in order to resemble you more and to save souls."

She was now so ill that they had once already administered Extreme Unction thinking that her release was at hand; she could no longer move without help; the sound of voices hurt her, she herself could scarcely speak a word without exhaustion. Yet she lingered on. Dreadful sickness now made it impossible for her to receive the Sacraments, to her the worst of all deprivations. At times she could only moan to God to take pity on her. At other times she could speak a little, and exhorted the Sister to answer "So much the better," every time she should complain of being in pain. To the Almoner, who asked her if she was resigned to dying, she replied that resignation was necessary only for living. On the eve of her death, when her sister Céline, now herself a nun, was sitting with her, she was gently pleased on seeing a dove fly in and perch by the open window.

It was the last earthly pleasure she knew, for by morning she was crying pitifully that she could not breathe this air and asking when she should breathe the air of heaven. Suddenly sitting straight up in bed, she who for weeks had been unable to move cried out, "The cup is full to the brim! No, I could never have believed it was possible to suffer so much. . . . I can explain it only by my extreme desire to save souls. . . . All that I have written about my desire for pain, oh, how true it is! I do not regret having given myself up to love."

By the evening she was asking if it was not the last agony, and on being told that it was, but that it might be prolonged by several hours, she murmured that she did not wish to suffer less. They were mistaken in their warning, for looking at her crucifix, she then uttered her last words, "I love Him. My God, I love you."

It was not long before mysterious scents of flowers began to be noticed in the convent, in places where no flowers were.

XII

THUS in complete obscurity, known only to a few, this little nun slipped away after a concealed and humble life and a death which in its way had been a martyrdom of the least dramatic type. Hundreds, thousands of nuns had lived similar lives, good, pure, devout; there was nothing to distinguish Sœur Thérèse de l'Enfant Jésus from their long procession. According to the custom of Carmel, her body was placed behind the grating of the choir, when all who were so minded might come to gaze once more upon the uncovered face; this exposition drew a large crowd, some of them attracted no doubt by a somewhat morbid curiosity, others by a more reverent affection for Thérèse in her early days or for members of her family. One rather curious incident took place, when a nun in repentance for having once spoken unkindly to Thérèse came to kneel by the bier, and, pressing her forehead against it, became aware that she was cured of a long-standing cerebral anaemia. Otherwise the last ceremonies took place as usual, with becoming lack of display, and a wooden cross was placed over the grave, bearing the words, "I want to spend my heaven doing good on earth."

A curiously complete parallel to her life and practices may be found in the brief story of Beatriz Oñez, a Carmelite nun professed at Valladolid in 1570; so complete that, but for the sequel, every word related of her might be applied to Thérèse. She was said never to utter a word with which fault could be found; never to make an excuse for herself, even though the Prioress would find fault with her for things she had not done. She never complained of anything, never by word or look did she hurt the feelings of anybody, never failed in obedience but did whatever she was commanded to do readily, perfectly, and with joy. The most trifling thing we do, she was wont to say, is beyond all price if we do it for the love of God. Her sufferings, which were very grievous, and most distressing pains, she bore willingly and joyfully, begging her sisters to pray that God might send her much suffering to make her happy; yet, when it came to her, kept it secret as far as she could, that those around her might not see how much she had to bear. Even in her death she resembled Thérèse, for she seemed as though gazing at something which filled her with gladness, and as her body was laid in the tomb a most powerful and sweet smell was perceived arising from it. Yet, for all this similarity, what honour has ever been paid on earth to Beatriz Oñez, who differed in no way from the equally inconspicuous Carmelite of Lisieux? Buried lives! their earthly record ended with the last shovelful of soil as their companions turned away to resume the daily sacrifice, the daily devotion.

All was over to outward appearances, but the most remarkable chapter in the history of Thérèse Martin was to open only after her death. Her life had been so sequestered, so uneventful, that her name would have remained unknown outside the small territory of Lisieux, and with the gradual falling-off of the few people who had known her the sea of forgetfulness would have closed for ever over her grave, but for the existence of that unstudied manuscript, l'Histoire d'une âme. Thérèse's last months on earth had made a profound impression on the Prioress, Mère Marie de Gonzague, who now reproached herself with certain harshness towards Thérèse in the past, and, contemplating with tears a picture of Thérèse as a child on her mother's knee, began to wonder how she could make amends. It is hard to resist the suspicion that Mère Marie de Gonzague had at moments been irritated by Sœur Thérèse, but death is a great obliterator. It will be remembered that it was customary to send a kind of obituary notice to all the other convents when a Carmelite died; it now occurred to the Prioress to print and distribute the Histoire, letting Thérèse speak for herself. How effectively she spoke can be estimated only by the startling results which ensued.

In the whole history of the Church, such a thing had never been known before. The book, first read in the convents, was then lent to chosen friends; the circles widened rapidly, and before long the

Carmel of Lisieux was inundated with orders for copies of the book
from all parts of France. Not only orders arrived, but numbers of
young women all desirous of entering the convent of Lisieux and
following in the footsteps of Thérèse de l'Enfant Jésus. From the
French provinces they came, and then from Ireland, Italy, Portugal,
Turkey, and even from the Argentine. As Lisieux, crowded out, could
not possibly cope with them all, they had to be distributed as best
they might into other convents wherever the Order possessed a
foundation. The value of the written word had never been more
clearly demonstrated than now, when it shot this searchlight beam
into the recesses of Thérèse Martin's obscurity.

It was not only impressionable or repentant young women who
found themselves attracted by Sœur Thérèse and the solution of her
Little Way, but priests and missionaries all over the world, some of
whom had started by being sceptical, declaring candidly that they
were put off if not actually repelled by her emollient sentimentality.
The youthful and critical seminarists of Bayeux, who now spent a
great deal of their time in argument about the merits or demerits
of the book and its author, were especially captious in their judg-
ments, but amongst them was a certain ill young abbé Anne, whose
doctors diagnosed galloping consumption and gave him at most a
few more days to live. A *neuvaine* to Thérèse was instantly begun (and
this alone shows how high her reputation already stood), but apparently to no avail: after some days of intercession it was thought that
the end would come during the night. Forewarned of this probability,
the young man, who, for all his piety, had no wish to die, pressed
a relic of the nun to his heart and passionately invoked her in silent
prayer, saying that although he felt sure she was in Heaven, he was on
earth where much work remained to be done, and that, in a word,
she must cure him.

An extraordinary change visibly taking place without delay in the
patient, the doctors were summoned in haste and to their astonishment
were obliged to declare that they found him completely restored to
health. Lest any exaggeration should be suspected, it is as well to
give the statement in the words of Lisieux' official chronicler in a
work crowned by the French Academy, "The destroyed and ravaged
lungs had been replaced by new lungs, carrying out their normal
functions and about to revive the entire organism. A slight emaciation
persists, which will disappear within a few days under a regularly

SAINT THÉRÈSE OF LISIEUX 167

assimilated diet." Moreover, not only did the abbé Anne make a
complete recovery from the ravages of this usually fatal disease,
which, as is well known, is especially pernicious in youth, but developed
in after-life a remarkably robust health and constitution. The miracle
was so well authenticated, owing to the attendance and the testimony
of the doctors, that it was later taken as one of the two test cases
demanded.

Without making any attempt to explain or to explain away such
phenomena, let us merely continue with a very brief list of instances
taken almost at random from the seven volumes entitled *A Rain of
Roses (Pluie de roses)*, edited by the Carmel of Lisieux. Thérèse's
promise that she would send down this shower when once she had
reached Heaven was being most multitudinously and variously fulfilled. There was the Bishop of the Upper Congo, who persuaded
her to cure a missionary attacked by sleeping sickness, and who,
although he had asked no favour for himself, was incidentally cured
likewise of his chronic and disabling rheumatism. There was the
Prioress of a Carmel in southern Italy who, having an urgent debt
to pay off, found the needed banknotes miraculously placed in an
empty drawer of her writing-table. There was the Reverend Alexander Grant of Edinburgh, a Presbyterian minister who, not content
with embracing the Catholic faith after his perusal of *l'Histoire d'une
âme*, uprooted himself from Scotland and went to live in Thérèse's
birth-house at Alençon, there to receive the increasing stream of
pilgrims. There was the manufacturer of Liverpool, a hard-bitten
man, who after reading the *Histoire*, caused a statue of Thérèse to be
placed in all his workshops, presented a copy of the book to all his
work-people, and, what they probably appreciated most of all, gave
them a week's holiday with full pay. Maurice de Waleffe, a sceptical
journalist, wrote in *Le Journal* that the world had fallen on its knees
before the purest soul since Francis of Assisi. To say that the world
had fallen on its knees was perhaps going rather far, but there was
no denying that the cult was growing at an extraordinary rate in
all countries and continents. It is perhaps not surprising to find her
venerated among the French Canadians, but somewhat unexpected
to meet with a similar enthusiasm in the industrial cities of the United
States. There, in the Protestant hospitals, the nurses and even the
doctors got into the way of advising their patients to invoke her aid.
The post-bag of Lisieux was swollen by requests for the *Histoire*,

for portraits of Thérèse, for scraps of relics, from Australia, Ceylon, India, South America, Spain, Italy, Germany, Austria, England, and all the time new tales of miraculous cures filtered in from the distant French colonies and from missions in Africa and the Far East.

It became increasingly evident that the popular clamour would soon demand some satisfaction, and the first steps towards obtaining it were taken by one of those young women who had presented herself at the gates of the Lisieux convent, and, being amongst the first comers, had obtained admission. She was a Breton, who, contrary to all preconceived ideas of that hardy though pious race, inclined strongly towards a social and elegant life, with an avowed contempt and pity for nuns and all their works. Illuminated suddenly by the *Histoire*, she abandoned her gay pleasures, proclaimed herself a "conquest of Sœur Thérèse," and became a postulant at the age of nineteen. She must have been rather precocious in worldly cynicism, or perhaps her experience had been unfortunate, for she wrote:

> J'allais avoir vingt ans; je connaissais le monde.
> Hélas! combien mon cœur était desenchanté!
> Au lieu d'un doux nectar pur et frais comme l'onde,
> C'est un brûlant poison qu'il m'avait presenté.

Yet her spiritual qualifications for the good life were evidently outstanding, for in spite of her youth she rose rapidly to the dignity of Prioress where she found herself at last in a position to promote her dearest wish, that of obtaining the Apostolic recognition of Thérèse's virtues. Unfortunately, as the official chronicler puts it, she had pushed her imitation of her celestial friend to the length of contracting consumption of the lungs and descended to the grave after seven years, but not before she had secured the co-operation of the newly elected Bishop of Bayeux, Monseigneur Lemonnier. The wheels of the vast, ancient, and complicated machine had begun to revolve.

After some delays, during which the volume of evidence continued to roll in through the doors of the episcopal palace, the Bishop finally received a reply from Rome, authorising him to begin his official investigation of the facts.

XIII

IT may be of interest at this point to scrutinise the procedure necessary before the honour of public *cultus* may be conferred, and to glance at the historical background of the qualifications which set the great machinery of Rome in movement on behalf of the little nun of Lisieux. Such honour is not bestowed without the most relentless examination, the rules having progressed in stringency since the early days of the Church when no formal ritual of canonisation obtained and *cultus* was awarded, especially to the martyrs, more or less by popular acclaim. The first instance of formal canonisation in fact does not occur until nearly a thousand years after the birth of Christ, when John XV conferred it on Ulric of Augsburg in 993, but another two hundred years were to elapse before Alexander III decreed that even the bishops could not exercise the right without submission to the Holy See. In those days of the twelfth and thirteenth centuries the process of canonisation could succeed very rapidly on the death of the person concerned, thus St. Thomas à Becket, St. Francis of Assisi, and St. Anthony of Padua received their title of Saint within three, two, and one years of their decease respectively. Teresa of Avila herself, some four hundred years later in date, had been raised to the fellowship within forty years of her death. To guard against possible abuses, for the Church of Rome is nothing if not cautious, the jurisdiction was gradually tightened up, and in the seventeenth century we find Urban VIII in two separate decrees going so far as to lay down the rule for an exact differentiation between the status of Blessed and Saint. Roughly speaking, a local bishop could authorise beatification carrying with it a local honouring or *cultus*, but canonisation could only be extended to the whole Church by the recognition of the Holy See. A period of fifty years, moreover, was fixed as the minimum before a cause of canonisation could be begun.

The stages in the hierarchy of sanctity are three in number: Veneration, Beatification, and Canonisation. The first stage may be skipped, but before canonisation may be conferred it is necessary that beatification should first be pronounced. Even for this second stage the conditions are sufficiently exacting: a general reputation for holiness, an heroic quality of the virtues, and the working of recognisable miracles. The privileges of the beatified, however, are relatively limited. No church may be dedicated to them, nor may they become patrons of nations, dioceses, or religious bodies; and their relics may be exposed only in churches where their Mass has been sanctioned. The canonised saint on the other hand is entitled to far wider honours. Benedict XIV who was Pope from 1740 to 1758 and is the authority on these matters, decreed amongst other things that the saints should be prayed *to* and not *for*; that their images should be adorned with the halo or other attributes of sanctity; and that their relics should be publicly honoured. Members of the Catholic Church are not compelled to believe in the miracles accepted in support of their claim to sanctity, but they *are* compelled to believe that every person duly canonised is now in Heaven, since the decision of the Church cannot be wrong and admits of no argument or divergent opinion. A little more latitude is allowed in the case of the merely beatified, when the obedient sons and daughters of the Church may decide for themselves whether or no the blessed one has reached Heaven, although they are warned that it would be "extremely rash not to do so." Before proceeding to canonisation, at least two miracles must have been worked since the elevation to the ranks of the Blessed. The rites of beatification take place in the great hall above the vestibule in St. Peter's, when the papal brief is merely read by the officiating bishop, but canonisation takes place with enormous ceremony in the basilica itself and is conducted by the Supreme Pontiff in person.

The precautions observed are many, especially in regard to the miracles. The medical point of view receives the utmost consideration. In the case of a healing, physicians, surgeons, and specialists are called as witnesses, and have to testify under oath that the alleged cure could not have taken place under natural laws. Their refusal to make this declaration leads to a rejection of the miracle, which will no longer be considered by the Congregation of Rites. All cases of auto-suggestion, hysteria, and epilepsy are automatically rejected; nor will any cure be accepted where a surgical operation has been performed, since it is held that the operation and not the intercession of the proposed saint may have been responsible. Similarly on the spiritual side, although heretics and even infidels may be admitted as witnesses, the father confessor is debarred, even though his penitent may have released him from the seal of confession. No shorthand is permitted, and all evidence must be taken in longhand by the notary. The cost of such proceedings is naturally very high, and in order to economise several causes may be considered simultaneously. Even the final ceremony of canonisation may take place jointly, as in the case of Teresa of Avila, St. Philip Neri, St. Francis Xavier, St. Isidore the Labourer, and St. Ignatius Loyola, who were all five canonised on the same day.

The actual examination of the claim is executed precisely in accordance with the disposition of a court of law. The procedure amounts to the presentation of a suit, before a jury which is the tribunal of the Congregation of Rites, a permanent commission of cardinals supported by subordinate officers and under the presidency of a Cardinal, but with the Pope in the background as supreme and ultimate judge. The proofs in support of the claim, which have first been very circumspectly assembled before presentation by the local bishop's court, are offered to the Roman court by a Postulator who in secular law would be termed the solicitor or counsel for the plaintiff. There is also a counsel for the defence, technically known as the Promoter of the Faith, but popularly as the Devil's advocate,— *advocatus diaboli*,—a term used by many people without any realisation of its true origin. His duty is to pick any holes he can find in the pleadings. Conversely, the Postulator is known as God's advocate, —*advocatus Dei*,—a term which for some reason has never passed into such general use, perhaps because human nature, or so it would appear, seems always to seize more gleefully upon the mischievous than upon the inspiriting theme.

Among the priests concerned in the enquiry on this occasion was a Vice-Postulator named Monseigneur de Teil, whom Thérèse had seen when he gave a lecture at her convent. He did not know that Thérèse had then exclaimed, "Is he not touchingly zealous! How happy one would be to point out some miracles to him!"

She had supplied him with plentiful miracles now. The case of the abbé Anne was considered, and also that of Sœur Louise de Saint Germain, who in her convent at the foot of the Pyrenees was dying of internal ulcers and had in fact received the Last Sacraments, when an intercession to Thérèse produced not only a vision of Thérèse herself and, some days later, a complete return to health, but also a strewing of rose petals of all colours round the patient's bed. No one knew how they had come there: they had arrived during the night. Moreover, on the eve of her exhumation Thérèse appeared to the Italian Carmelite Prioress whose debt had been so opportunely provided for, and informed her that nothing but her bones would be found in her grave. The Prioress was quite unaware that any exhumation was about to take place, but learnt afterwards that her ghostly visitor had spoken correctly.

The very strange case of another Theresa must be mentioned here, not only on account of its own inherent interest but also on account of its association with Thérèse of Lisieux. This concerns the well-known Theresa Neumann, a peasant girl of Konnersreuth in Bavaria. To all appearances Theresa, or "Resl" Neumann, was a very ordinary and rather stupid child, one of ten children in a healthy family, and herself so strong that when working on a farm she could carry sacks of flour weighing over a hundred and fifty pounds from the cellar up to the third floor. Nothing abnormal here. When Resl was nineteen, however, a series of accidents, culminating in total blindness, rendered her completely helpless; and before long she began to suffer from cramps and convulsions so violent that on one occasion all the teeth in her upper jaw were broken. She, so robust, was now bedridden and incapable of standing alone. The doctors marvelled that she could remain alive at all. They had given up all hope of doing anything for her, but it was the turn of Sœur Thérèse to intervene. Resl had a great devotion to Sœur Thérèse, a devotion which was to be rewarded by no less than seven miraculous cures. The first one was perhaps the most dramatic, though the other six, which included the straightening of her twisted leg, the restoration of the power to walk, the disappearance of all symptoms of sudden and acute appendicitis, and the cure of pneumo-bronchitis when the prayers for the dying had already been begun, were sensational enough. But on the first occasion, Resl, who had just been preparing a novena in honour of Thérèse's beatification, woke in the morning to find herself as usual unable to see. Then, she says, she felt as though someone were touching her pillow, and, raising her eyes, she was surprised to see her own hands and the picture of Thérèse of Lisieux hanging on the wall. Her sister came into the room, but as she had not beheld her for four years she could recognise her only by her voice. The entry of another sister caused Resl to exclaim "Is it believable that you have grown so much*"

Thérèse during one of her appearances had announced that her rain of roses would become a torrent, and with the outbreak of war in 1914 her legend grew in proportion to the fulfilment of her promise. The French army adopted her extensively as their special protector. "It is true that we have Jeanne d'Arc," wrote one soldier, "but the little Sister is nearer to us." Whole regiments placed themselves under her protection. Gun batteries were called after her. Men going into battle carried her medal on their persons. Pilots, including the ace Bourjade, either called their aircraft Sœur Thérèse or decorated it with her portrait. Meanwhile the enormous process of enquiry lumbered on, undisturbed by war, taking seven years (from 1910 to 1917) to reach its first conclusion, a period of time which is perhaps less surprising when we learn that the preliminary report ran to five thousand pages after a hundred and nine sessions of many hours each. During the apostolic process at Rome a further ninety-one sittings took place, resulting in a dossier of two thousand five hundred pages.

XIV

THE Church, always thorough, had been in no hurry, but finally Cardinal Vico, Prefect of the Congregation of Rites, remarked that they had better hasten to glorify the little saint, if they did not want the voice of the peoples to run ahead of them. In the early days of the Church, he said, where beatification was accorded by popular acclaim, Sœur Thérèse would long since have become Blessèd. It was a fact that petitions from all quarters of the world were now pouring into the Vatican; Brazil sent a processional reliquary of gold and precious stones, and some 80,000 pilgrims flooded Lisieux annually with visits to her tomb, a number which before long was to increase to 300,000. It would be wearisome to follow the stages in detail to that crowning ceremony which took place on May 17th, 1925, or even

* See appendix, p. 178.

to record the various authenticated miracles which were submitted to the examination of the Congregation of Rites. It suffices to mention two amongst the many which took place immediately after the beatification, the first a Belgian girl brought in a dying condition to the tomb where she was instantly cured of pulmonary and intestinal consumption; the second a nun of Parma, cured through intercession of arthritis and spinal tuberculosis.

There was room for a congregation of only fifty thousand in the Basilica of St. Peter's, but over two hundred thousand applications for seats were received. Thirty-four Cardinals, over two hundred Archbishops and Bishops, and an enormous concourse of priests, prelates, members of the religious Orders, and Apostolic Notaries preceded the banner of the new saint down the brilliantly lit aisle under innumerable garlands of Thérèse's roses, succeeded by the arrival of the Pope, borne to his throne in front of the Chair of St. Peter. The roaring crowd was silenced only by the command to stand while Peter should speak through the lips of Pius. Strange, awesome ritual of this Church with all its hierarchy, tradition, power, splendour and organisation, so self-contained within the framework of the temporal realms of this world, so immutable, so secret in its workings among the hearts of millions, so apparent in its majesty on such occasions of affirmation in its Roman stronghold! As the Basilica had risen by the banks of the pagan Tiber, as the genius of Michaelangelo and Bernini had devoted itself to the glorification of God at the command of the Vatican, so had the strange and magnificent institution which is the Church of Rome, both visible and invisible, risen from the small peasant beginnings of the carpenter's shop and the fishing boats of Galilee. The company of twelve men, brown and barefooted, had swollen into the company of the Princes of the Church, grave and billowing in their silks of red and purple, with their immense authority and the unrestricted apparatus of pomp. Yet in the underlying spirit there was no difference at all.

When all was over, when the Te Deum had been sung, when three white roses had without recognisable cause floated down from a pilaster and settled themselves at the right hand of the Pope, when the Cardinals had made their traditional offerings of doves and pigeons in gilded cages, or wine and water in little kegs of silver and gold, when Mass had been celebrated and all the dignitaries had withdrawn, the great temple was left open to the irruption of the crowd that blackened the piazza outside. All day long the lights burned, but when the evening came, the warm soft evening of a Roman May, an even more splendid spectacle delighted the Roman people and the half-million strangers surging in pilgrimage into the Eternal City. Not since 1870 when another child of France received a similar honour at the hands of Pius IX, had such a spectacle been offered. Illuminated by thousands and thousands of candles outlining the cupola, the façade, and Bernini's colonnades, the apparent conflagration of the Basilica was reflected even into the waters of the Tiber, much as the humble signpost candle of Thérèse's Little Way was now throwing its beam along the darkness of a troubled world.

Not long after the ferment in Rome had died down, a more modest and perhaps more touching procession wound its way, carrying indigenous relics, into the little garden of Les Buissonnets.

Appendices

✥

ST. JOSEPH OF CUPERTINO

(*See pp.* 53, 57)

THE remarkable case of this Italian saint (1603–1663) is regarded as a classic example of attested levitation. His mentality was extremely simple; his intellectual achievements were confined to reading with difficulty and writing with even more difficulty; as a boy he was known in his village as the gaper (*Bocca aperta*); he was so absent-minded that he forgot to eat; at the various trades to which he was apprenticed he got into perpetual trouble, partly owing to his clumsiness and partly to his forgetfulness. There seemed nothing left for him but the religious life, which at first he pursued in the humblest capacity as a lay-brother, though even then he could not be trusted to carry a pile of plates without dropping them or to remember to light the kitchen fire. Later, through sheer luck and the casualness of the examiners, he was ordained as a priest. But in this capacity, for other reasons, he had to be prevented from fulfilling his duties. He could not be allowed to say Mass, to take part in processions, or even to share in the meals of the community, for at any moment he was apt to rise into the air and remain suspended for a long time. They tried hitting him and burning him and pricking him with needles, but once he had passed out of his senses nothing would bring him back to them except sometimes a sharp order from his Superior. The accounts of his flights are numerous and amazing; some of them doubtless have gained in the telling, but the residue, related by eye-witnesses, makes up a story sufficient to satisfy the curious. Among the less credible tales is the account of his picking up "as though it were a straw" a cross thirty-six feet high and too heavy for ten men to lift, and flying with it in his arms to set it in its place. He frequently flew up to holy statues in order to embrace them, and, carrying them off their stands, floated about with them; he sometimes picked up a fellow-friar and carried him round the room; on one occasion the sight of a lamb in the garden sent him into such an ecstasy, thinking of the Lamb of God, that he caught up the little creature and rose with it into the air. The lamb was probably not much alarmed for it was said of this simple though surprising saint that all animals had an instinctive trust of him, the sheep especially coming round to listen to his prayers.

Amongst his other peculiarities, he had the habit of uttering a shrill cry, like a bird, on taking flight.

St. Agnes of Montepulciano (1268–1317), not content with leaving the ground when she went into ecstasy, was frequently seen with her cloak covered with manna, "looking as if she had been out of doors in a heavy snowstorm."

The Rev. Herbert Thurston, S.J., most cautious and sceptical of investigators, personally described to the present writer the case of a priest of his acquaintance, who was obliged to weight the soles of his boots with lead in order to keep himself down while saying Mass. But, as Father Thurston remarked, it did seem puzzling that a little extra weight should make all that difference to a supernatural power capable of lifting a man's body without any difficulty.

THE BURNT AND WOUNDED HEART

(See p. 100)

A SOMEWHAT similar case is recorded of Maria Villani (died in 1670), but with the surprising factor that this nun had herself drawn a diagram to illustrate the wound made in her heart by a fiery spear. The external wound was visible during her lifetime, and was several times examined and probed by three different Dominican fathers who signed formal depositions describing their findings. Nine hours after death had taken place, the body was opened, when bright blood gushed forth, and so much heat proceeded from the heart that the surgeon was obliged to withdraw his hand several times

M

before he could finally grasp the heart and extract it. It was then seen to exhibit a wound exactly in accordance with the drawing made by the dead woman, and moreover "the lips of the wound are hard and seared, just as happens when the cautery is used."

THERESA NEUMANN

(See p. 172)

THUS far the interventions of Thérèse, which were accompanied by many appearances and locutions, but this brief account of Theresa Neumann would not be complete without the rounding-off of her subsequent history. Restored more or less to health,—that is to say, she could now walk and see,—she began to have intense visions of Christ's Passion. These visions before long were accompanied by physical signs on her own body: blood streamed from her side and from her eyes; marks corresponding to a crown of thorns appeared upon her head; a red bruise, not actually bleeding, but oozing blood, appeared upon her right shoulder as though from the angular weight of a heavy burden; weals, as though from scourging, covered her body; and the stigmata appeared in her hands and feet. Here, in the place of the nails, pieces of hard flesh, like plugs, filled the holes. When photographed, the wounds in the hands revealed a bright surrounding light. These manifestations, whatever their cause, are associated with a physical anguish that innumerable eyewitnesses and medical men declare could not possibly be so terribly and convincingly feigned. It is also claimed that after the climax of the Good Friday's vision, when, she has watched Christ's body droop upon the Cross, and her own body has drooped with it, her mouth falling half open, her limbs relaxed and motionless, her heart for five minutes actually ceases to beat.

This is not the end of the perplexing tale of Theresa Neumann. It is, apparently, a fact, checked by the most careful supervision, that for many years she neither ate nor drank, much as she would have liked to do so. In spite of this total abstinence, and an almost equivalent lack of sleep, she loses no weight except on Fridays when her visions regularly occur (with special agony and intensity on Good Friday) when she loses from five to eight pounds, regained the following day. The sceptical may be tempted to dismiss her case as one of extreme auto-suggestion. But apart from the theological and scientific care taken in examining the evidence, a few curious facts appear to weaken this theory. Thus, in a case of auto-suggestion working on a very simple and unimaginative mind, one might expect the visions to run exactly on lines originating in something already known, already taught. On the contrary, Theresa Neumann insists on differing on many points from the orthodox version. For example she declares that the Cross, as carried by our Lord, was not in the usual shape, but consisted of four separate pieces of wood tied together, and that on arrival at Calvary the two longer pieces were joined end to end, and the two shorter pieces joined at acute angles, forming the letter Y. She insists also our Lord's feet were at only about a yard from the ground. Again, her idea of the Magi does not correspond to any picture or story she might have seen or heard, for according to her account the Christ-child was no swaddled baby but was already eighteen months old when the Kings arrived in Bethlehem, and, just learning to walk, was able politely to escort them to the door at the end of their visit.

It should be related also that she recognised Aramaic as the language of the shepherds; differentiated between the Aramaic spoken by an educated man like Pilate and the popular speech of the Apostles; used the Pyrenean dialect in describing the apparition of our Lady at Lourdes; and recognised Portuguese as the language she had heard spoken by St. Anthony who, although called of Padua, happened to be a native of Lisbon.

One last fact in connexion with Theresa Neumann may be noted: her birthplace was not far from that of Adolf Hitler, who, brooking no rival in the intuitive regions, suppressed her and her thousands of pilgrims and her prophecies in 1934. In support of this action on the part of the Führer, it is said that some of her prophecies were of a most discouraging character concerning himself and his own career.

It is necessary to add that the Church has by no means accepted her experiences and revelations as being of divine origin.

While on the subject of Theresa Neumann, it is not irrelevant to mention the cases of the Florentine St. Catherine dei Ricci (1522–1590) and of Blessed Stefana Quinzani (1457–1530). St. Catherine, a nun in the Dominican convent of San Vincenzio at Prato, occasioned much inconvenience to her fellow-inmates by the ecstasies into which she entered weekly for twelve years, and which attracted crowds of importunate visitors to the convent. These ecstasies had the peculiarity that besides mentally contemplating the scenes of our Lord's Passion she also enacted them in her own person. Losing consciousness with the greatest regularity at midday on Thursday, and regaining it at four o'clock on Friday afternoon, she followed in gesture, scene by scene, the visions which were taking place in "the eyes of the soul." Thus, at the moment of the arrest in Gethsemane, she would stretch out her arms as though offering her hands to be bound; when the moment came for our Lord to be roped to the pillar for the scourging she would stand stiffly upright; later, she would bow her head to accept the crown of thorns. Although deprived of her senses during these performances, she would nevertheless address the sisters of the community with exhortations displaying "a knowledge and loftiness of thought and eloquence not to be expected from a woman."

Like Theresa Neumann, she received the stigmata.

Blessed Stefana Quinzani, who came from Brescia, likewise enacted the scenes of the Passion every Friday. Twenty-one eye-witnesses signed a document describing the occurrence. Like St. Catherine, she would reproduce the actions of our Lord during the scourging, the crowning with thorns, and the nailing to the Cross. The stigmata would appear on her hands and feet; she would become completely rigid, and although the onlookers exerted all their strength they were unable to alter the position she had adopted or to bend a single joint of her limbs. On extending her arms during the scene of the Crucifixion, her left arm was observed to be stretched considerably beyond its natural length, resembling in this the arm of St. Catherine of Genoa which was said to gain five inches in similar circumstances.

It may be left to the reader to make what he can of these and similar manifestations.

CE QUE J'AIMAI . . .

A literal translation

(*See p.* 116)

Oh, how I love the memory
Of the blessed days of my childhood!
To preserve the flower of my innocence
Our Lord surrounded me always
With love.

I loved the barley-fields, the plain;
I loved the distant hill;
In my happiness, I scarcely breathed
As I harvested with my sisters
The flowers.

I loved the white daisy,
The walks on Sundays,
The light bird warbling on the branch,
And the lovely radiant blue
Of the heavens.

O Memory, you give me repose . . .
You recall many things to me . . .
The evening meal, the scent of roses,
Les Buissonnets full of gaiety
In summer.

These are only a few stanzas from the poem which contains fifty-two stanzas.

THE PRAYER OF FRANCE TO JEANNE D'ARC

A literal translation

(See p. 144)

Oh Jeanne, remember your country,
Your valleys enamelled with flowers.
Remember the laughing meadow
That you left in order to dry my tears.
Oh Jeanne, remember that you saved France.
Like an angel from Heaven you cured my sufferings.
    Listen in the night,
        To France lamenting.
            Remember!

Remember your brilliant victories,
The blessed days of Reims and Orleans;
Remember that you covered with glory
In God's name the kingdom of the Franks.
Now, far from you, I suffer and sigh.
Come to save me once more, Jeanne, gentle martyr!
        Condescend to strike off my iron bonds . . .
        Remember the ills I have suffered.

I come to you, my arms loaded with chains,
My brow veiled, my eyes bathed in tears;
I am no longer great among the queens,
And my children water me with grief.
God is nothing to them now! They desert their mother!
Oh Jeanne, take pity on my bitter sorrow.
        Return, great-hearted daughter,
        Liberating angel,
            I trust in you.